GOLF *by* DESIGN

GOLF *by* DESIGN

How to Lower Your Score by Reading the Features of a Course

BY ROBERT TRENT JONES, JR.

Foreword by Tom Watson

Little, Brown and Company

Boston   New York   Toronto   London

Copyright © 1993 by Robert Trent Jones, Jr.

First Edition

Library of Congress Cataloging-in-Publication Data
Jones, Robert Trent, Jr.
    Golf by design : how to lower your score by reading the features of a course /
by Robert Trent Jones, Jr. — 1st ed.
                        p.   cm.
    ISBN 0-316-47298-0
    1. Golf.   2. Golf courses.   I. Title.
GV965.J58   1993
796.352 — dc20   93-16807

10 9 8 7 6 5 4 3 2 1

IMAGO

Book and cover designed by Arias Associates Design, Palo Alto, California
This book was set in Adobe Centaur and Adobe Bembo.

Published simultaneously in Canada by Little, Brown & Company (Canada) Limited

Printed in Hong Kong

Cover Photo: Henebry Photography

The photographs in this book are used through the courtesy of the following:
Leon Bird, p. 88; Rob Brown, p. 236; Henebry Photography, pp. ii, xii, 2, 7, 22, 24, 30, 34,
44, 58, 64, 66, 72, 85, 93, 100, 109, 117, 121, 122, 127, 130, 136, 157, 162, 178, 192, 197, 228,
231, 261, 270; Chris John Photography, p. vi; Leonard Kamsler, pp. 102, 150; John Knight,
pp. 135, 167; Brian Morgan Photography, pp. 60, 141, 164, 176, 207, 226; Larry Petrillo, p. 174;
Tony Roberts Photography, pp. 9, 27, 29, 33, 38, 50, 78, 142, 144, 186, 194, 213, 216, 218,
234, 238, 242, 245, 248, 254, 264-265, 267; Dick Severino ©The Irish Collection, p. 18;
Steve Szurlej, p. 170; C. Patricia Williams, p. 97; Terry Husebye, Back Cover.

To My Mother and Father
and All Those Who Love the Game of Golf

THE ROBERT TRENT JONES GOLF CLUB, LAKE MANASSAS, VIRGINIA

CONTENTS

Golf attracts more players than any other outdoor sport. No doubt there are almost as many reasons for this as there are players, but one reason is certainly shared by all. It's the simple pleasure of being on a beautiful course.

No other game combines the wonders of nature with the discipline of sport in such carefully planned ways. A great golf course both frees and challenges a player's mind.

At the same time that your spirits lift with the sunshine sparkling on leaves, water, and new-mown grass, you also must confront what the unique combination of nature, landscaper's art, and your kind of game can mean on a particular course. That combination is the subject of this book. To talk about the *design* of a course means much more than how it is laid out or where the bushes are planted. *Design* is also a way of thinking about how to play.

Several years ago, I was pleased to collaborate with Bob and Sandy Tatum to design the Links at Spanish Bay in Pebble Beach, California. During the process, I was able to see firsthand how Bob took into account factors such as the prevailing wind, grass types, and the illusion possibilities based on the links character of the site.

In *Golf by Design,* Bob takes off his designer's hat and puts on a player's cap to show you not how to design a course, but how to design your game — how your shot selection and execution should take into account golf course features. This lesson benefits enormously from the insights Bob has into this game from his long career as a leading golf course architect.

This book is packed with useful detail. You will return to it time and again. Discussions of bunker types, illusion techniques, and the psychological elements of hazards are extremely informative. Detailed analysis of the green shows why there really aren't any "gimmies."

Bob's experience-based explanations will increase any golfer's understanding of the functions and attributes of golf course features. This increased awareness can pinpoint the features that are most important on a given shot and can concentrate a player's attention on the key elements. The result will be a more decisive shot selection and the kind of execution that is critical for players to lower their scores.

Most golfers look at their courses with a mixture of pleasure and nervous anticipation. *Golf by Design* will help you see the course in a new, more confident way and will enhance your appreciation of both its natural and designed elements.

Better yet, it will improve your game.

Tom Watson

Late one afternoon, during a U.S. Open, Ben Hogan was on the practice range. An astute observer remarked that he was drawing the ball rather than hitting his legendary controlled fade. Hogan responded by picking up a map of the golf course, what we golf designers commonly call a "route plan." He silently indicated locations of key features and the many holes that were routed from right to left, requiring exactly the shot Hogan was perfecting. His in-depth study of the route plan gave him an edge even before the tournament had begun.

Jack Nicklaus helped popularize another aspect of golf course analysis. Until the 1960s, most professional golfers relied heavily on their own sense of distance and their caddie's insight to help them in club selection. Nicklaus began meticulously studying courses before playing them, walking off distances himself, and then having his caddie, Angelo Argea, double-check them in order to produce a "book" of precise measurements and notes on how each hole should be attacked. Gradually, other professionals began to follow this procedure, and yardage books are commonplace today for both pros and amateurs alike.

In the summer of 1984, Seve Ballesteros strode confidently to the eighteenth green on the Old Course at St. Andrews. Moments earlier, Ballesteros had been visibly concerned about his club selection for the approach shot to the 354-yard par-4 finishing hole of the British Open Championship. All that stood between the talented Spaniard and the trophy was the Valley of Sin.

Ballesteros knew that if he left his approach shot below the huge undulation in the green, a bogey and ensuing playoff were distinct possibilities. With a breeze gusting in his face, he selected a pitching wedge, enough club to carry the hump but not so much as to risk overshooting the green, which was bordered by a fence and the out-of-bounds. A skilled wind player, Ballesteros judged the shot perfectly, the ball finishing 12 feet below the cup.

He then holed the putt for his second Open championship.

These are three examples of how top players devised strategies to beat the challenge posed by the golf course designer. By studying the integral parts of a golf hole, they maximized their chances for scoring success.

This book will not teach you how to design a golf course any more than an art book teaches you to paint like Picasso. It will, on the other hand, give you a good understanding of golf course "features," in which I include a multitude of factors to consider, ranging from green and bunker types to wind and illusions. This understanding will improve your game by making your shot selection more decisive and raising your confidence level. This is what I refer to as playing "golf by design."

Try this quick quiz to see how well equipped you are to analyze a hole:

1. What are three of a designer's favorite optical illusions?

2. What do the mowing patterns on a course show you?

3. How can bunkers be friendly?

4. What is the invisible hazard on a golf course?

If you can't answer all these questions, you will benefit from *Golf by Design.*

This book will provide a guided tour of the elements you can expect to encounter on a course. Along the way, we will devise playing strategies for the tee, fairway, bunkers, greens, and other features, like illusions and wind. Course-management techniques will also be developed for analyzing and approaching particular features. Finally, we will use these strategies and techniques to attack some classic holes.

Each chapter is set up for easy comprehension with drawings, pictures, and charts to help you grasp key concepts. I've included technical analysis and strategic evaluations you can put into practice right away. Beginners can use this book to help build a solid foundation for their game, while experienced golfers will refresh their knowledge of sound course management. Whatever your skill level, I know that *Golf by Design* will lower your score.

Robert Trent Jones, Jr.
Palo Alto, California

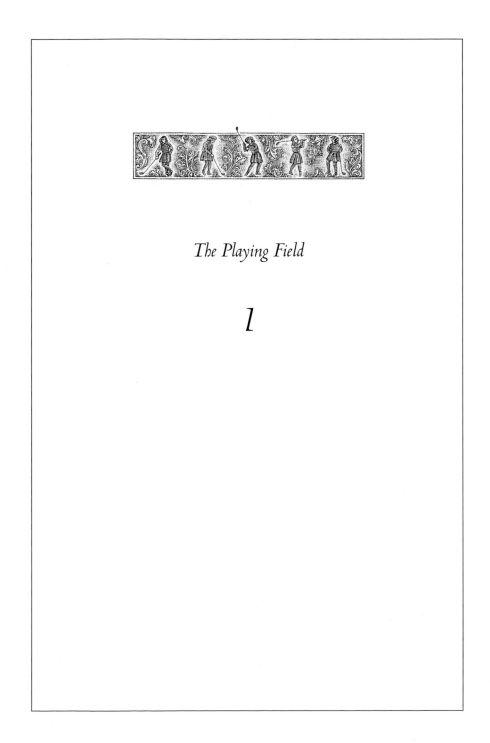

The Playing Field

1

WELL-DESIGNED HOLES, SUCH AS THE
PAR-5 FIRST AT ZUIRYO GOLF CLUB IN JAPAN,
OFFER SEVERAL OPTIONS OF ATTACK.

PRECEDING PAGE:
THE PAR-4 SIXTEENTH HOLE AT POIPU
BAY GOLF RESORT IN KAUAI, HAWAII, BLENDS
NATURALLY WITH THE EXISTING TERRAIN.

 Golf has a playing field like no other in the world. Mountaineers, hunters, fishermen, trekkers, cyclists, and scuba divers may command the most extensive locales in which to pursue their challenges, but among the games that require a formal playing field, golf offers an unusual combination of rigid specifications mixed with sometimes wild and unpredictable irregularities of nature. In other words, no two courses or rounds are ever so alike that you can attack them with exactly the same game plan. For me, the constantly changing conditions and the infinite variety of holes define the essence of the game.

To perform successfully on such a playing field demands a mindset that can quickly analyze the features of a course, including changeable elements like weather and wind, and that can then decide what challenge the architect poses. In every case, there is a risk-reward factor. The course forces you to evaluate each shot in terms of nerve and skill. The more decisive your shot selection and thought process, the greater your chances of mastering the course.

One way to understand how a designer envisions a course is to look at other sporting activities. For example, when I design a course, I have in mind chess, pool, auto racing, and certain target sports.

Chess

Chess is intrinsically a game of attack and defend. Like chess, golf is a silent battle — give or take a few eruptions — in which the architect assumes the role of defender against the golfer attacking the course. Imagine a well-defended golf hole as a giant chessboard where the designer has created a system of defenses. They can be as obvious as a waste bunker or as subtle as a mound or a contour in a putting surface. The designer not only places obstacles on a hole but also may camouflage them. A good rule for playing golf, then, is to start each hole aware that there may be subtle, mysterious, or even hidden elements waiting to sabotage your game.

Much like a game of chess, a golf hole requires strategic planning to improve your score.

Your attack on a hole involves land and air strikes. From a land perspective, visualize yourself threading a path through the defenses in search of the best landing and takeoff areas, much the way ground troops move from position to position when assaulting an enemy fortification.

Obviously, attacking a hole by air is a major weapon in your arsenal. Be aware also that designers employ illusions, prevailing wind currents, and landscape to challenge your attack. Simply getting the ball into the air isn't enough if it lands in the wrong place.

Thinking about golf as a giant chess game played between designer and golfer will help you understand the need for long- and short-range strategies. Chess masters are great because they have a custom-made strategy for each opponent. You need the same for each hole and each course.

If you think the pros play a different game, you're right. They ask numerous strategic questions before they see a new course and often rely on caddies to scout the most subtle nuances. Practice rounds are used to probe the design, and holes are analyzed shot by shot after each round. Nick Faldo of England and Bernhard Langer of Germany are two outstanding professionals who leave nothing to chance. Faldo walks the course without clubs to study its characteristics, while oftentimes Langer measures every hole with a yardage wheel to get exact calculations to and from features before hitting a practice shot.

Pool

Golf is colloquially referred to as "pasture pool." Pool proficiency requires mastery of spins and angles and skill in organizing a sequence of shots. Winning depends heavily on sound, strategic thinking. Champion pool players, such as Minnesota Fats or Steve Mizerak, know how to manipulate the cue ball with spin. Their wizardry includes almost perfect control of all angles on a pool table.

Golf is also a game of spins and angles. Pros talk of "working" the ball. Technically, this means imparting various spins so that while the ball is airborne it moves toward the chosen target and rolls advantageously when it lands. Working includes the skills of fading, drawing, stopping the ball, and making shots bounce forward.

While a well-made pool table is a perfectly planed surface, a golf hole can be seen as a field of hundreds of angled planes, which can

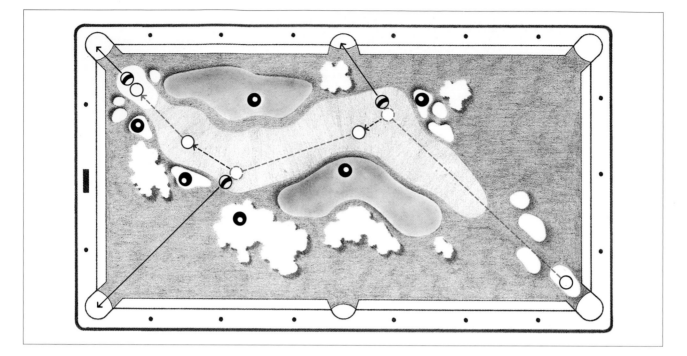

Similar to pool, golf is a game of position, where players strive for preferred "leaves" and the best angle to the target.

deflect the ball in various directions. Visualize a hole as a series of planes without grass, trees, and water. That's the designer's view when he lays out a hole.

Like pool, golf is primarily a game of position. The professional pool player never takes one shot at a time. He organizes a series of shots in his mind in order to sink all the balls on the table. The key is to get a good "leave," or an ideal position for the next shot.

Ask yourself how often you look at a hole in terms of the best leaves for subsequent shots. The value of such positioning is that you begin to tailor your shot-making abilities to the course. You mentally take control of the design. This strategy is not restricted to tee shots. Playing approach shots to the "fat," or safe, side of greens instead of at the flag may reduce your score dramatically. Designers try to tempt you into hitting risky shots. Smart players know their limits and avoid trouble.

THE WATER-LINED PAR-4 EIGHTEENTH
HOLE AT DORAL COUNTRY CLUB IN MIAMI,
FLORIDA, IS PLAYABLE FOR ANY GOLFER,
PROVIDED YOU CHOOSE THE PROPER ROUTE.

For example, consider the 437-yard par-4 eighteenth hole at Doral Country Club in Miami, designed by Dick Wilson and nicknamed the Blue Monster. Because of its configuration, low-handicap players normally will choose a route off the tee that is close to the water, significantly shortening the hole. Mid-handicappers and high-handicappers should play away from the water on their tee shot. For their approach, mid-handicappers may attempt to reach the green's right-hand side while less skilled players may elect to lay up short of the water fronting the green.

During the Greater Ozarks Open at the Highland Springs Country Club in Springfield, Missouri, I was paired in the pro-am with professional Bob Lunn and three other amateurs. On the 430-yard par-4 seventh hole, a dogleg left around a large lake, Lunn played close to the water and attacked the flagstick with no fear of the lake. I drove down the right side of the fairway, taking the water out of play. One of my playing partners, a stocky fellow with a healthy handicap, attempted to follow Lunn's route. He wound up wet.

Auto Racing

Golf is also similar to auto racing in several ways. All top drivers have heroic courage and a special talent for shifting gears to match the racecourse. Indianapolis 500 winner Danny Sullivan, an avid golfer, noted the parallels during an AT&T Pebble Beach Pro-Am. "I look for the curves and banks on a golf course the way I do when I drive a race car," he said. "If you aren't aware of them, they can ruin your day."

A golf hole starts out like a straightaway, with the golfer flooring it (swinging aggressively) on most par-4s and par-5s for distance. Then he downshifts (approach shot), eases up on the accelerator for a hairpin turn (chip), and guides the car (ball) across the finish line (into the hole). It's an ongoing adventure to get the most from your car or clubs without pushing too hard.

ACCOMPLISHED GOLFERS LIKE RAYMOND
FLOYD ALWAYS FORMULATE A GAME PLAN FOR EACH
HOLE AND PLAY TO THEIR STRENGTHS.

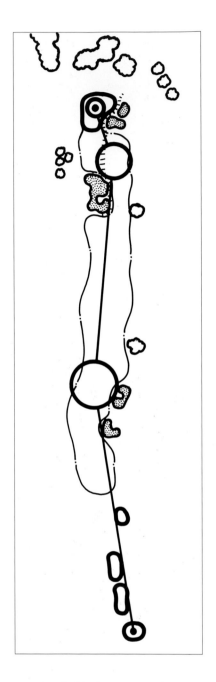

Holes like the par-5 second at Wailea Golf Resort's Gold Course on Maui, Hawaii, can be separated into a series of defined target areas.

If players are not mentally conditioned, they will fail to master the course. Venues like the U.S. Open are the ultimate test of patience and perseverance. When Tony Jacklin won the 1970 U.S. Open at Hazeltine National in Minnesota, friends taped the word TEMPO on his locker before the final round. Despite slick greens, thick rough, and windy conditions, Jacklin was able to adjust his game and maintain composure throughout the five-hour ordeal. All pros know that rhythm and positive thinking are essential to winning. Just ask their sports psychologists.

On certain holes, a designer may attempt to upset a golfer's balance and mindset. He tempts you to push too hard or take unnecessary chances. I often say, "Lost ball, lost stroke, lost confidence."

Target Sports

A final comparison can be made with target sports. To understand target golf, we must examine the evolution of shot making. Golf started as a knockabout affair in which players advanced the ball with a stick toward an endpoint, the early game being played mostly on the ground. Technical advances in ball construction, club making, and swing mechanics produced a higher shot trajectory, and the game moved from a land campaign to an aerial assault.

The consequences have been twofold. First, golfers today watch pros shoot "darts" from great distances and often believe that is the only way to play the game. Second, on many modern courses, targeted areas have been designed and maintained to receive high-trajectory shots.

Someday golfers may enjoy even greater distances, although it's hard to imagine anyone hitting a ball farther than John Daly. When astronaut Alan Shephard hit his famous shot on the moon on February 5, 1971, Walter Cronkite of CBS television said, "Soon, we'll have a Robert Trent Jones course on the moon for Alan to play." If I ever get to build it, we'll name it Moonscape

Golf Course and it will play about 40,000 yards from the back tees. That should keep Daly on his toes.

One way to view a golf hole is as a series of defined target areas. In the illustration of the 520-yard par-5 second hole at Wailea's Gold Course on Maui, Hawaii, I have taken a par-5 hole and outlined archery-like bull's-eyes in various spots. With your tee shot you can aim for a reasonably large landing area, say 20 to 30 yards in diameter, whereas hitting into the green from 100 yards, you should be trying for an area 20 to 30 feet in diameter.

I encourage every golfer to consider separating some holes into a series of par-3s to better visualize the hole as a group of distinct targets. Note the diagram of the par-4 hole. Player A sees a 250-yard par-3 and a 140-yard par-3, while Player B sees a 200-yard par-3 and a 190-yard par-3. Each player proceeds with a specific target in mind on each stroke, and the prudent golfer will avoid trouble and play within his ability level.

This approach played a key role in Raymond Floyd's victory at the 1986 U.S. Open at Shinnecock Hills Golf Club in Southampton, New York. At the 513-yard par-5 sixteenth hole, Floyd played two accurate shots to intermediate targets and left himself in perfect shape for a short iron to the green — one of his strengths. Floyd made a birdie and clinched the championship, becoming the oldest U.S. Open winner, which proves that position and smarts can often outwit length and youth.

Design Styles: Strategic, Penal, and Heroic

The terms "strategic," "penal," and "heroic" frequently are applied to shots, features, holes, and even entire courses. Because these shorthand references appear in various places in this book, it is important for you to understand how I will be using them. It is equally important to understand that these categories are not

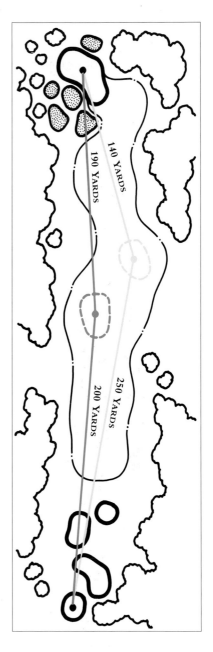

If you visualize each shot as a par-3, your ideal landing area becomes more apparent.

11

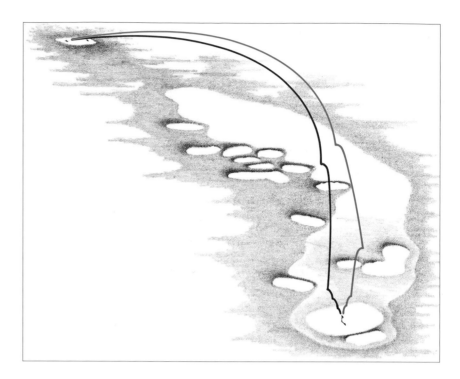

totally clear-cut in every case, and experts may disagree regarding which term best describes a specific hole, shot, or feature.

For me, a "strategic" hole is one that has at least one reasonable route for reaching the green in regulation with very little risk of incurring a severe penalty because of a misplayed shot. In addition, if there are several alternative routes, the route having the greatest distance generally has the least risk of incurring a severe penalty for a misplayed shot.

A hole is "penal" if the only way to reach the green in regulation involves successfully executing at least one shot that will incur a severe penalty if misplayed. This shot itself can also correctly be referred to as being penal. Often the severe penalty involves a ball lost in an escape-proof hazard like water, a ravine, or out-of-bounds.

A "heroic" hole has at least two distinctly different alternatives for reaching the green in regulation. One lacks a severe penalty for a misplayed shot. With the second, however, a misplay incurs a severe penalty, but, if successfully negotiated, it will reward the player with a far superior position and/or distance advantage. Thus, the player faces a truly heroic decision. This shot itself also can be called heroic.

Accomplished designers often blend strategic, penal, and heroic holes to create a golf course with a pleasing balance and rhythm, much in the same way that a composer constructs a symphony. Although well-versed players may vehemently disagree over which of the three categories a particular hole belongs to, it would be rare indeed for them to classify all holes on a given course as strategic, penal, or heroic. Therefore, when an entire course is given one of these labels, it likely means that it has a relatively large number of holes of that particular type.

Last, hazards are frequently referred to as being penal. This appellation simply indicates that the hazard is one from which escape is extremely difficult or impossible. Additionally, hazards can be classified as strategic. This label is usually applied to hazards that are well positioned and from which a full recovery shot is possible. You will never hear hazards being called heroic.

I am sure that you have recognized that, in many ways, a heroic shot decision can be by far the most complex and nerve-racking. It represents the essence of great mental golf: a clear choice offering obvious but very different risks and rewards.

Now that you have an idea of what a hole needs to have to be strategic, penal, or heroic, let's look at examples of each type. The holes I have selected can clearly be placed in one of these three categories.

The 444-yard par-4 eighth hole at Muirfield Golf Club in Scotland is a classic strategic hole. As the sketch shows, it is a dogleg right with a series of fairway bunkers guarding the right side of the fairway. Long hitters can reduce yardage by cutting the corner

*Penal holes such as the
par-3 seventeenth at the Tournament
Players Club Stadium Course
in Ponte Vedra, Florida,
have no options.*

but must contend with the bunkers. Short hitters or intermediate players can play to the left side of the fairway the entire length of the hole and avoid sand, but this strategy results in a longer second shot to reach the green.

An excellent example of a penal hole is the 132-yard par-3 seventeenth hole at the Tournament Players Club in Ponte Vedra, Florida, a demanding layout designed by Pete Dye, that plays host to the Players Championship. As the drawing shows, a successful shot on this par-3 must avoid water everywhere. Any stroke that is short, long, or off line will end up in Davy Jones's locker. The hole and the shot are clearly penal because no other route exists to reach the green.

The 540-yard par-5 eighteenth hole at Pebble Beach Golf Links in California is universally regarded as one of golf's truly heroic holes. It features not one but a pair of heroic choices generated by the presence of the Pacific Ocean down the entire left-hand side. As you can see from the sketch, the tee shot can be played over as much water as you dare to improve your angle and shorten the distance to the green. Your second shot also can take the brave line over another corner of the ocean, with considerable distance and angle reward if successful. Alternatively, you can follow a safer route along the right side of the hole, at the expense of having to cover a greater distance.

In conclusion, the designer orchestrates the hazards and other features into mental and physical playing challenges whose product is holes that are strategic, penal, or heroic.

GOLF COURSE SETTINGS

In my view, there are six geographic categories of courses: links or seaside, prairie, parkland, desert, mountain, and tropical. Your first lesson in course mastery is to be aware of the significant

natural factors that should influence how you approach a course. Obviously, areas have common characteristics, but it is the specific combination of factors that gives each geographic category a distinctive identity.

Links or Seaside Courses

Like most golfers, my first journey to the game's fountainhead in Scotland was an emotional experience. Standing on the first tee at the Old Course in St. Andrews, in the shadow of the Royal and Ancient clubhouse with its weathered stone, I steadied myself against the wind and the withering gaze of onlookers curious to see how visitors play their first shot. Having previously studied the layout, I looked down the wide double fairways of No. 1 and No. 18 and played my tee shot inward, away from the out-of-bounds and the ocean. Knowing how the Old Course was laid out, I had decided on this approach long before I saw the first hole. My playing partner, however, aimed directly toward the green and sliced out-of-bounds on the right. Then he greatly overcompensated and hit a vicious pull-hook way to the left through the first and eighteenth fairways, again incredibly out-of-bounds. After I explained the proper strategy to him, he fared better. As connoisseurs know, the trick to playing the Old Course is to aim shots inward, which results in tougher approaches but avoids unplayable lies in the heather and gorse on the boundaries.

Classic courses such as St. Andrews tend to hold a grip on the imaginations and attitudes of those who play them. Because of history and tradition, there is a sense of reverence for the game played here. You feel as if you're walking on sacred and mystic ground. To wit, at the Old Course, fourteen holes (Nos. 2 and 16 through Nos. 8 and 10) are served by double greens. Curiously, when the hole numbers of each set of double greens are combined they add up to 18, the traditional number of holes on a course. I have no idea what it means, but who am I to question the superstitions of the Scots.

St. Andrews is built on "linksland" — the sandy, undulating hills or dunes formed along a coastline by wind and waves. Other celebrated links courses, like Royal Dornoch in Scotland, are located on rolling sandy terrain adjacent to estuaries. Links courses are notable for a number of reasons. To golfers raised on parkland or mountain courses, links courses lack apparent definition. The tremendous openness of the seaside setting does not provide natural markers, such as trees and hills, that golfers usually rely on to judge distance. The effect is a certain disorientation that made a friend lament, "You play a links course by Braille — with fourteen clubs, a white cane, and a trusty seeing-eye dog."

Don't look for symmetry at Ballybunion Golf Club in Ireland or the Turnberry Golf Courses in Scotland. The early players and designers were inclined to follow natural paths in the earth, rather than superimpose a routing plan, and that was the game pure and simple. To give themselves a better chance, they played between the dunes and out of the wind.

Links courses have an irregular quality about them. As you walk them your feet begin to feel the many bumps and rolls, and the hidden swales reveal more contour than expected. The ground traditionally is firm, sharp bounces are common, and tiny pot bunkers excruciating. Lately, however, as five-time British Open champion Tom Watson has pointed out, the installation and extensive use of modern irrigation systems have made many links courses much lusher, thereby softening them and, in the process, compromising some of their unique playing characteristics.

Generally, links courses feature indigenous fescue grass, which tends to produce tight (thin) lies. Fescue rough tends to be swirly and light, and playing out of it generally is fairly easy due to its light clubhead resistance. However, the other forms of rough encountered on a links course are an entirely different story. Rely on a caddie or local member to help you decide if you can extract your ball from infamous gorse and heather. When in doubt, use a lofted club and play to the fairway. It will save you strokes and ligaments.

A friend played Royal County Down in Northern Ireland. On the 440-yard par-4 fifth hole, he pushed his drive into tall fescue grass and gorse on the right, and the foursome spent considerable time looking for the ball. Finally, his caddie found it but then couldn't find the bag, having laid it down in the high rough during the search. An inauspicious start to say the least.

Links courses rely heavily on wind to provide part of the challenge. Some would argue that seaside courses without wind are relatively

THE PAR-4 ELEVENTH HOLE AT
BALLYBUNION GOLF CLUB'S OLD
COURSE IS CHARACTERISTIC OF
EARLY LINKS COURSES THAT FOLLOW
THE NATURAL MOVEMENT OF THE LAND.

tame. When Faldo won the British Open at St. Andrews in 1990, incredibly, the wind did not blow during any rounds, resulting in unusually low scoring. Conversely, when a gale wind kicks up — the norm — woe to the golfer who can't keep the ball low or hit punch shots. You have not played a links course unless you've jousted with the wind. Spaniard Seve Ballesteros can attest that the wind frequently emerges as the victor. At Muirfield in the 1987 British Open, Seve needed three full shots and a short iron to reach the green on the 558-yard par-5 fifth. Ballesteros is a man who reaches most par-5s in two, often with a driver and a long iron.

Success on seaside courses often depends on your ability to gauge winds. I usually ask a local golfer about wind currents so I can "align" shots more effectively. Good players actually try to bank shots off crosswinds, like a pilot angling a plane during a cross-wind landing. The effective distance into the wind on a given hole often leaves newcomers incredulous. For example, a 9-iron shot on a windless day may call for a 3-iron in a gale. Caddies often say, "The yardage is a bit longer today, sir. We have a two-club wind." That means you need to add two clubs to carry the distance.

From a shot-making standpoint, the low, along-the-ground, bump-and-run and knockdown shots are necessary weapons on a properly maintained links course. Under true links conditions, being able to keep the ball low and run it to the hole will definitely help your score. During the process of winning the 1972 British Open at Muirfield, Lee Trevino, a native Texan, used a Texas wedge (a putter) around the greens to combat the firm ground and wind.

Prairie Courses

Prairie courses are cousins to inland heath courses, which were off-shoots of the original linksland courses. Until the second half of the nineteenth century, links seemed to be the only terrain that could support a proper golf hole. Attempts to build on clay soils failed because greens were rock hard in summer and mushy in winter. Finally, someone recognized that heathland, which shares important drainage similarities with links, was almost ideal for laying out a course.

On the American side, prairies are located in the region known as the Great Plains. Some well-known prairie courses are Oak Tree's East Course (Oklahoma) and Prairie Dunes (Kansas). My father's design at Hazeltine National (Minnesota) and my own at Oxbow Country Club (North Dakota) illustrate the genre. Outside the U.S., you will find prairie courses bordered by rich farmland in areas such as the pampas (grasslands) of Argentina, the Transkei of South Africa, and, of course, in Australia.

When I play prairie courses, I always keep in mind that they are similar to links courses in a number of respects. For example, they are susceptible to winds, often fierce, from different directions. If the situation dictates, you should favor low, running shots — assuming the design affords an open entry to the green. It's basically decisiveness and feel.

While growing up in the metropolitan New York area, I occasionally played at Winged Foot Golf Club in Mamaroneck, New York, with club professional Dave Marr. Many courses in Texas, where Marr was raised, feature prairie-like conditions. One day at Winged Foot, Marr used his putter around the greens, much as Trevino did at Muirfield, and had great success. From then on, I looked for ways to use this effective shot.

Great Plains courses are in Big Sky country, where looming horizon influences perception. Accordingly, you should determine distances incrementally by breaking a hole into small parts and locating intermediate markers you can judge with accuracy. An edge of a bunker, a rise in a mound, or another notable landmark can help you determine the length of your shot. Or, ask a caddie or a local player for yardages.

Prairie courses are in regions subject to radical and surprising weather changes, ranging from sudden, sharp winds, cold spells, severe thunderstorms, and tornadoes, to searing heat, which debilitates even the strongest players. Temperatures can change dramatically in the span of a few minutes, affecting everything from the distance the ball carries to the amount of clothing you may need. Such courses require the ability to adjust to the elements — often several times during the round — to perform at your best.

Parkland Courses

When the courses moved inland from the sea and began to be carved out of North American woods and forests, the first parkland-style courses were created. Ron Whitten, *Golf Digest* Architecture Editor, chose a parkland setting for the magazine's "armchair architect" design contest, because he knew that most golfers would identify with a site that contained elevation changes, trees, and water. In the United States, parkland courses are concentrated most heavily in the Northeast (Winged Foot Golf Club and Merion Golf Club), the Southeast (Augusta National Golf Club), the Midwest (Medinah Country Club), and the Northwest (Eugene Country Club). Many parkland courses (Pine Lake Golf Club and Onuma Golf Club) are also found in Japan.

Trees are an integral part of the playing challenge. On the plus side, they act as perceptual guides for the players. But they also can be penal hazards, which force you to take additional strokes and incur penalties. They also obscure vision and hide other features of a course. Courses cut from heavy tree stands have a "chute" feeling. Keeping your driver in the bag is often sound strategy.

Grasses frequently are heavy and lush, often providing good lies in the fairway. On the downside, because of clay soil, more moisture, and sodden turf, you tend to get less roll, especially in the rough.

THE PAR-4 SEVENTH HOLE AT UNIVERSITY RIDGE GOLF COURSE IN MADISON, WISCONSIN, DISPLAYS PRAIRIE CHARACTERISTICS.

Fairways frequently are sweeping, with a rolling character. You can use these contours to your advantage. On the other hand, rolling slopes force you to consider intended landing areas carefully because shots frequently finish on sidehill angles or roll into unforeseen difficulties. Gauging roll accurately is important — unless you're proficient swinging on one foot or enjoy chipping out of trouble.

One significant factor on a parkland course is the character of the wind, which is usually a zephyr, as contrasted with a gusty seaside breeze. When the woods are cleared to create fairways, some pockets are left that amplify and redirect the wind with a boomerang effect, causing it to swirl and making it difficult to judge distance and determine ball movement along a flight path. When such winds are present, be extra careful to evaluate their force and effect. One trick is to scan the tops of trees for movement. Sometimes you can't feel it, and other times it comes from a totally unexpected direction.

Desert Courses

At one time, deserts were perceived as poor sites for golf courses. But new irrigation, earth-moving, and maintenance techniques now give designers more options. Topographically speaking, deserts are predominantly level but can feature noticeable elevation changes when located near mountains. A prime example is the Mountain Course at the La Quinta Hotel Golf Club near Palm Springs, California. While the site is mainly flat, many holes are nestled against mountains and offer deceptive uphill and downhill transitions not normally associated with desert courses. Areas of inland California, the Southwest, and Florida have similar terrain. Surprisingly, Florida has many courses with desert characteristics, such as little variation in topography combined with sandy soil.

One such desert locale was the Royal Rabat course in Morocco, where my father and I had an experience that illustrates the theory of attack and defend as it relates to the construction of a golf course. The site was an army encampment, so we were asked to give a briefing to the soldiers, who were going to build the King's course. We were taken into a tent where our routing plans had been hung on a board, as if they were sketches for a military campaign. In effect, they were, because the plan encapsulated our defensive strategies for the course.

When playing a desert course, be aware that designers often work overtime creating features in these settings. For example, nonindigenous grasses for fairways and greens are specified by the designer;

lakes are also manufactured for visual contrast and improved aesthetics. In some cases, designers go to extremes to relieve flatness by creating elevations, including mounds that offer both obstructions and crazy caroms.

The desert sun produces an intensity of light and shadow that can distort perception. The shimmering heat sometimes creates a mirage effect. Therefore, you should double-check objects to ascertain exactly how far away they are. The warm air is usually still and dry. Also remember that desert air, like mountain air, is thin, so allow for extra distance. On the other hand, you may encounter cold air pockets that can deaden shots in the early morning or twilight hours.

Desert fairways and greens have two common characteristics. Due to the sandy composition of the soil, the conditions of both these areas are very firm. Additionally, the intense sunlight combined with today's irrigation systems allows for a healthy growth of turf grass, which can be tightly manicured. Together, these factors result in extra bounce and roll, thus increasing distance. However, the extra roll can make your short-game and recovery play more difficult, due to reduced control in stopping the ball on the greens.

In states like Arizona, where water for irrigation is at a premium and governmental limitations on the amount of playable acreage are present, designers are often forced into creating tight, narrow courses. These constraints are heightened by the fact that desert rough and transition areas are difficult to recover from. In this regard a desert course mirrors a links in that areas off the fairway contain native vegetation. Additional fieldwork is required to discover which growths are playable (avoid the jumping choro cactus). Those who ignore this advice are destined to lose strokes, clubs, or clothing.

Desert courses are sometimes situated on rising plateaus near the foothills of mountain ranges. Frequently, coyotes think they're

CACTUS AND NATIVE VEGETATION ABOUND ON THE PAR-4 THIRTEENTH HOLE AT DESERT MOUNTAIN'S GERONIMO COURSE IN SCOTTSDALE, ARIZONA.

members. In addition to dramatic backdrops, these arid mountains offer the designer options for creating contour, elevation, and perception puzzles. Errant shots will often find rock outcroppings and reptiles as well.

Mountain Courses

For sheer beauty, probably nothing compares to mountain courses. I've designed courses on sites from the North American Rockies to the French Alps and the rugged mountains of Japan, and I love the challenge. Maybe that's because I'm a skier and like the thrill and excitement of downhill runs, especially on slopes that can leave you on your derrière.

Mountain courses feature dramatic changes in elevation and often give players the feeling of negotiating a slalom course. Like a testy hill, these courses are exhilarating but require precision and clear thinking. If you get too caught up in the scenery, disaster is inevitable. Because of the topography, many holes are routed through narrow canyons, and accuracy is a must. Don't hesitate to sacrifice yardage for direction. It's easier to take a lesser club than hunt for an errant 300-yard drive.

Mountains mean water, often twisting, crystalline streams. Most designers try to integrate them into the routing. Occasionally, streams will be difficult to see, so check the scorecard for maps. At the course I designed in Steamboat Springs, Colorado, the rushing Fish Creek comes into play on many holes, acting as a perilous water motif.

Situated at heights, mountain courses can produce a loss of balance, a sort of golfing vertigo. This reaction may be subtle but can affect club selection. The added elevation means thinner air and shortness of breath. Shots will travel farther. The rule of thumb is 2 percent for every 1,000 feet of elevation, but, if possible, test this rule on the practice range before you play.

DRAMATIC BACKDROPS ARE COMMON ON MOUNTAIN COURSES LIKE KEYSTONE RANCH RESORT IN KEYSTONE, COLORADO.

Probably the most critical factor in playing a mountain course is deception: things are not as they seem. At my father's El Rincón Club in Bogotá, Colombia, and my design in Keystone, Colorado, distances and dimensions seem quite different at elevations of approximately 9,000 feet. You can be sure the designer of a mountain course will use this perceptual difference to his advantage. Again, be aware of these potentially deceptive features, and see if you can solve their mysteries on the practice range before you start your round.

Tropical Courses

Tropical courses are something I know well, and I've got the insect bites to prove it. I've worked on more than twenty-five tropical sites, from the Caribbean islands to the jungles of Mexico, Southeast Asia, and the South Pacific. Unlike desert environments, where there is sparse vegetation and trees, the forests and jungles pose opposite problems for designers and golfers. In many tropical areas, particularly the islands of the Caribbean, Hawaii, and the South Pacific, trade winds affect the design of holes.

Lush vegetation forces designers to use special techniques for routing holes. It also changes the composition of grasses and the way the ball plays off them. Grasses in these parts of the world — such as kuchgrass, elephant grass, and zoysia — can be as tough as wire brushes. Throughout the tropics, the native grasses frequently pose much greater golfing challenges than are encountered in more temperate climates.

Many jungles grow on mountains, so courses built here combine mountain and jungle environments. For example, at our Four Seasons Resort course on the island of Nevis in the Caribbean, errant shots end up in jungle ravines bordering fairways. On the courses I've done in Malaysia and the Philippines, what I call "edges" (the natural areas just off the fairway) would be easier to attack

HUMIDITY AND DENSE VEGETATION MAKE TROPICAL COURSES LIKE CANLUBANG IN LAGUNA, PHILIPPINES, A CHALLENGE TO DESIGN AND PLAY.

31

with a machete than a 5-iron and offer practically no hope of recovery. Accuracy is mandatory unless you like snakes.

Jungle environments conceal dangerous obstacles that magnify the challenge and excitement. You never know what you'll encounter. At Royal Selangor Golf Club in Kuala Lumpur, Malaysia, wild monkeys have sometimes chased golfers. In certain areas, various reptiles reside in the foliage adjacent to tees and greens. On some courses in Asia you'll find a local rule that provides: "A player may remove a ball two club lengths from a coiled cobra or sleeping tiger without penalty of death." He may also run like a scared jackrabbit.

Maintenance on tropical courses is often difficult, so be prepared to play in less than perfect conditions. Grass can grow uncontrollably and sporadically in these regions, causing a variety of lies.

As you can see, golf courses have many faces, depending on where they are built. To succeed on a particular course, you must know the territory and its specific conditions, and adjust your game plan accordingly. Now let's go to the first tee, where your round begins.

THE FIRST AND EIGHTEENTH
FAIRWAYS ON THE OLD COURSE AT
ST. ANDREWS, SCOTLAND,
RUN TOGETHER AS ONE.

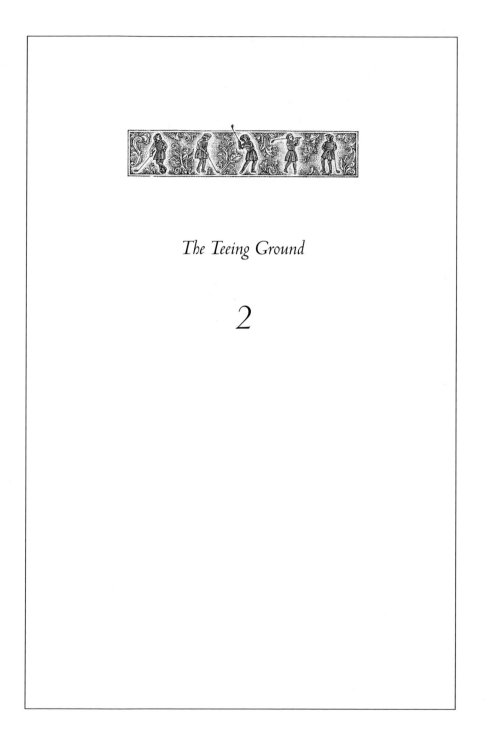

The Teeing Ground

2

Properly aligned tees, like the par-4 first hole
at Glencoe's Glen Forest course in Alberta, Canada,
can help orient you to the preferred landing area.

PRECEDING PAGE:
THE PAR-4 TWELFTH HOLE AT HIGHLAND
SPRINGS COUNTRY CLUB IN SPRINGFIELD, MISSOURI,
FEATURES A FREE-FORM TEE COMPLEX.

Every tee is a new beginning and an opportunity to place the ball in an ideal position. Your performance off the tee generally determines how well you will play a given hole. Let's see how you can maximize your chances for greater success.

The tee is the one area on the golf course that gives you the best opportunity to control the playing conditions and variables, because you are assured of a perfect lie and a relatively level stance, and you can determine the best angle to the target based upon your skill level. Once you leave the tee, you are essentially at the mercy of the golf course, so use it to your advantage. With little exception, the tee sets the tone for what lies ahead.

To make the most of the tee, you must understand both its physical traits and its relationship to the overall hole. This knowledge is even more critical today, because after a long period of slow evolution, tremendous changes have occurred in the tee's physical and strategic importance during the last thirty to forty years.

Several years ago, as I stood perched atop a Hawaiian bluff that offered breathtaking vistas of the Na Pali Mountains, the Pacific Ocean, and the ravines and dense tropical vegetation below, I knew I'd found the perfect spot for the first tee. It afforded a panorama of the entire property as well as a clear view of the landing area — a spectacular starting point for our Prince Course at Princeville on the garden island of Kauai.

This opening hole shows how a tee shot can present a puzzle to average and expert players alike. The solution involves determining where to position your tee shot to obtain the desired approach to the green. The tees are elevated, and the hole generally plays downwind. Anini Stream, which snakes diagonally across the fairway and crisscrosses in front of the green, creates a number of challenges. On the right is a heavily verdant, steep embankment. Factoring in these two challenges, you should position the ideal

tee shot as far down the fairway as possible, avoiding the trouble that lurks on both sides. But remember, the tee shot must be straight, and your second shot cannot be made with a machete. With five teeing areas, the hole plays from 346 to 448 yards, meaning all players will be tested, regardless of their ability.

I always try to give golfers a chance to pick the set of tees that suits their game. The yardage differential between the championship and middle tees on the Prince Course is 788 yards. Despite what your ego tells you, the extra 40-plus yards per hole could be the difference between an enjoyable round and a visit to the local chiropractor.

Another elevated tee example is found on the 508-yard, par-5 first hole at Riviera Country Club in Pacific Palisades, California, site of the Los Angeles Open. The first tee is positioned more than 50 feet above the fairway, which is initially a confidence builder, because you don't have to worry about getting the ball airborne. But your confidence is short-lived as you begin to focus on the narrow fairway framed by the out-of-bounds left and the trees right (it appears tighter than it actually is). You will quickly perceive that the noticeable drop from tee to fairway will magnify any mistake you make with your line. The designer has used elevation to tempt you into swinging hard, with the potentially disastrous consequences of an off-line shot. Unless the shot is struck accurately, you will end up in serious trouble or hopelessly out of position for your second shot.

Instead of an elevation-based puzzle, the first tee at the Augusta National Golf Club in Georgia presents golfers with a bending challenge. The opening hole is a 400-yard par-4, slight dogleg right. Typical of Augusta, you will observe a wide fairway defined only by a large bunker on the right, but no distinct target for your tee shot. However, in this case, the rectangular tee is your reference point. The edges of the tee serve to align you in the

AT SKYLAND GOLF RESORT'S PAR-4 THIRTEENTH IN CRESTED BUTTE, COLORADO, THE DRAMATIC ELEVATION CHANGE FROM TEE TO FAIRWAY RESULTS IN INCREASED DISTANCE, BUT ACCURACY IS A MUST.

proper direction, much as the edges of a runway define the line of takeoff for an airplane.

These examples illustrate some of the selection challenges designers incorporate into a teeing area. Today's tee is the result of an extensive process of refinement in terms of function and appearance, bearing little resemblance to its rudimentary predecessors. Understanding its style and shape will help you formulate the correct strategy to begin any given hole.

The world's first written Rules of Golf, drawn up in Leith, Scotland, in 1744, stated that "You must Tee your Ball, within a Club's Length of the Hole." Gradually the Rules were modified and players moved a short distance from the hole to an adjacent area that served as a teeing ground. Many of these starting points were so poorly defined that golfers were simply required to select a spot within a certain number of club lengths from the previous hole to continue play.

Golfers would create a "high point" on which to place the ball with some sand taken from the prior cup while retrieving the ball or by making an indentation in the soil with the heel of their shoe or clubhead. Eventually, the tee area began to take shape in the form of a small square, or "teebox," as it was called. Yet these early teeing grounds remained generally nondescript areas and provided little or no orientation as to the proper direction or the most appropriate landing areas of the hole. Thus, players often found it very difficult to align their tee shots.

The tee largely remained a nonstrategic element until the end of the nineteenth century when a golf professional/golf architect, Willie Park, provided insight for its location and shape, pointing out that "tees should be placed on level parts of the course if possible, with a slight slope upward in the direction to be played." His statement was pertinent for three reasons: (I) it was important to have a reasonably level lie on the tee; (2) the slight upslope was a way to help players get the ball in the air; and (3) proper alignment of the tee was an essential factor for future architects to consider.

Park's ideas helped to formulate the criteria for new and improved teeing surfaces in the early 1900s as architects began to further understand the importance of the tee's physical attributes as well as its relationship to the rest of the hole. They started to realize that the teeing surface should not be a random spot chosen by each player but a distinct starting point for beginning the hole and helping players become properly oriented toward the correct target. The edges of the tees, both at the front and on the sides, were developed in a more definitive manner so as to align with the specific landing area.

On courses such as Pine Valley in Clementon, New Jersey, designers further evolved the tee by dividing the surface into a number of smaller teeing areas that provided players with various starting points. These smaller areas were the first signs that golf courses could be set up to challenge players of different skill levels and, more important, that various tee positions could dramatically change the target or landing areas. In many cases, the entire strategy of a hole would be dictated by the tee selected, and golfers would be forced to consider their options instead of mindlessly attacking a hole.

After World War II, the teeing area underwent further modification, largely due to the work of my father. It should be noted that by this time golf designers had been accepted as creative artists who sculpted pieces of property into playable golfing facilities. As for my father, he had been designing courses for more than a decade and was developing his own concepts in the process.

He became known for positioning features in the landing areas off the tee to make accuracy as important as distance. Oftentimes, however, when these features were located to challenge long-hitting expert players, they penalized only a small percentage of the most skilled golfers. My father realized that the way to make these features defend against all calibers of player was to build tees that created a wide variety of distance within the teeing area. Thus, he started to design tees as long, straight areas that became known as runway or "aircraft carrier" tees. The longer versions were often 50 to 60 yards in length and were intended to accommodate three sets of tees for beginning, intermediate, and expert players. Gene Sarazen joked that my father had a chronic crick in his neck from looking backward over his left shoulder for additional tee space.

A runway tee creates an amazing visual effect for the player. When properly aligned, the perimeters of the tee point directly at the preferred landing area, which is generally near a major hazard or obstacle, such as a fairway bunker. Regardless of which teeing area

*At Coral Ridge Country Club in Fort
Lauderdale, Florida, runway tees are a trademark
of this Robert Trent Jones Sr. design.*

you have selected based on your skill and length, the tee should aim you toward the proper target. From the post-World War II period up to the early 1960s, many architects followed my father's example and designed tees incorporating the runway concept with minor variations. Most teeing areas built during this period reflect some form of his thinking.

Proper maintenance techniques by the golf course superintendent have served to highlight the directional effects of these teeing areas. Two common practices that the superintendent employs are (1) mowing patterns on the teeing surface itself and (2) a noticeable cut of rough to accentuate the perimeters. As a player, you have the option to use either the runway or the edges of the tee to ensure precise alignment. This technique results in a visual flight path for your tee shot similar to that of an airplane taking off straight and true into the sky. Improper contact often results in a word called "Fore!" Or in the case of pilots, "Mayday!"

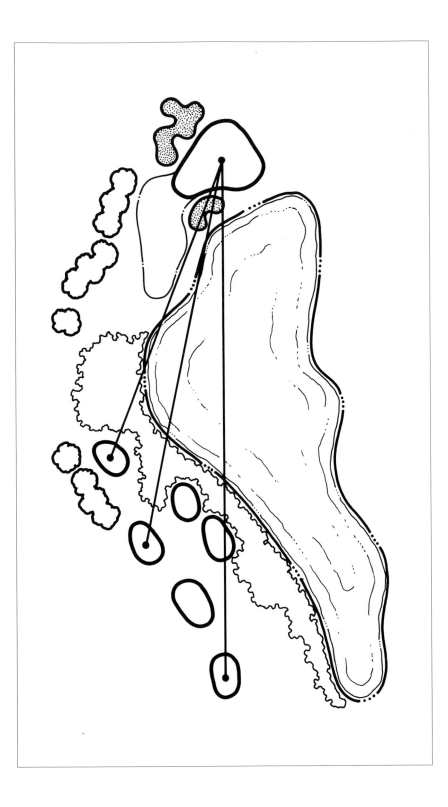

*At Squaw Creek Resort
in California, the par-3 sixth hole
features a series of staggered
tees that will test golfers
of all abilities.*

By the early 1960s, designers were refining teeing surfaces even further and developing new techniques to make the starting point of a golf hole more interesting. They began to experiment with the best ideas from the early 1900s combined with the concept of variable teeing locations from the runway era. Results were dramatic. Multiple teeing surfaces began to appear on new courses, and many older courses upgraded their teeing areas to take advantage of this combination of ideas. Noticeable changes were evident in the increased distances between tees on a single hole. Designers also found that, by adjusting the elevation of the tee slightly, they could create improved visual effects for the player.

The search continued for new ways to shape a tee, and soon designers discovered that they could control the look and feel of a hole through new configurations and improved maintenance techniques. They also began to reexamine their theories on tee placement and sought to find areas on a given piece of terrain that would allow tees to appear natural in relation to the surrounding landscape. Sensitivity to elevation change, distance, setting, and shape became commonplace.

During the past fifteen years, designers have taken the teeing area even further. Most of the golf courses built in the last decade contain elaborate teeing complexes that reflect a variety of shapes, sizes, and elevations. Designers go to great lengths to create many playing angles and distances to a variety of target areas by strategically positioning multiple tees.

The modern tee, properly designed and constructed, blends into the natural landscape. Today the creativity of tee configuration knows no limitations, ranging from a single row to a staggered series around the edge of a lake. Despite this great variation, the basic objective remains the same: challenging players of all skill levels.

The golfer who brings a game plan to the first tee almost always has a better round. If the greatest players in the world spend time analyzing the course in detail before they tee off, it makes sense for you to do the same.

Tommy Armour once told me, "There are no blind holes the second time you play them." He was right, but the first time you obviously have no prior experience playing a hole, so be extra careful. Once on the tee you have only a brief period to formulate a plan. It will be very helpful if you have studied in advance a route plan of the course. Oftentimes you'll find a route plan or an aerial photograph in the clubhouse. Reviewing this material can provide you with valuable advance information.

In addition to the route plan, two other basic tools will help you more effectively analyze a course before and during a round. They are the scorecard and the yardage book. Each tool can help you improve your performance before you ever hit a shot.

What a Scorecard Can Teach You

The scorecard is an excellent tool with which to analyze a course before you see it. For purposes of illustration, I've included the scorecard from my course at Brookside Country Club in Stockton, California. This particular card shows (1) the final route plan on the back of the card, indicating the shape and the physical characteristics of the holes, (2) the areas of water that come into play on eleven holes, (3) the location of the bunkers in the landing areas and target zones, and (4) the yardages from the three sets of tees. These are some of the main features at Brookside. Always try to identify influential characteristics of a course before teeing off.

HOLE	1	2	3	4	5	6	7	8	9	OUT
BLUE	390	418	160	531	396	335	587	163	450	3430
WHITE	367	396	122	512	372	301	556	126	427	3179
HANDICAP	11	5	15	9	3	13	7	17	1	
PAR	4	4	3	5	4	4	5	3	4	36
RED	272	316	86	452	298	248	464	91	318	2545
HANDICAP	11	3	15	7	9	13	1	17	5	
DATE:				SCORER:						

PLAYER	10	11	12	13	14	15	16	17	18	IN	TOT	HANDICAP	NET SCORE
	548	380	131	387	152	420	559	181	532	3290	6720		
	503	347	113	353	141	401	530	165	512	3065	6244		
	14	8	18	4	16	6	2	10	12				
	5	4	3	4	3	4	5	3	5	36	72		
	434	264	74	295	89	342	444	115	420	2477	5022		
	10	12	18	6	16	4	2	14	8				
ATTEST:													

The scorecard from Brookside Country Club in Stockton, California, contains useful information that should be studied before your round.

What you don't see on this card is wind direction. Try to determine how the winds blow and then note where you think they will be a factor. At Brookside, the prevailing wind blows from the northwest, and the storm wind comes out of the southwest. If this information were available on the scorecard, you would have a better idea of the shot-making challenges you can expect to confront.

Yardages: The scorecard shows yardages from championship, regular, and forward tees. On some courses, there may be four or five sets of yardages. At this point you have the important option of playing a forward or a back tee. Each set of tees is designed appropriately to challenge your shot-making skills. In this case, 6,720 yards (championship) is 476 yards longer than the regular tees (6,244), an average of 26 yards per hole.

On many newer courses, all measurements are made in a precise fashion using a laser technique and are marked on sprinkler heads.

This common knowledge can help eliminate indecision prior to selecting a club and allow you to focus on the vital design elements of the golf course.

Par: Par at Brookside is 36-36-72. There are five par-3s (all short to medium in length from the white tees), three of them on the back nine, which may mean an easier time coming home. Now you have your first fix on the overall rhythm of the course. The three par-3s on the back are balanced by three par-5s, each more than 500 yards. Thus, an educated guess says the front nine should play tougher, so gear up mentally right away.

Hole Handicaps: Handicaps can help you anticipate the relative difficulty of individual holes. On every scorecard, holes are ranked from 1 to 18, with 1 generally being the most difficult and 18 the easiest. Look for hard stretches of holes, or sharp swings from very hard to easy and back again, which could upset your playing rhythm. At Brookside, you can see that we start easy and finish hard on the front nine. The back opens with two relatively easy holes and then gets testy in the middle. Knowing the personality of a course will help your mental preparation.

Slope Rating: This scale indicates the overall difficulty of the course. Virtually all courses fall between the rating values of 70 (easiest) and 150 (toughest). For example, in the area where I reside, Northern California, the member courses of the Northern California Golf Association run from a low of 67 to a high of 147. If you have never seen Brookside and notice that its slope rating is 118 from the middle tees, you quickly realize that you face a medium test. Conversely, the slope rating at my father's Spyglass Hill Golf Course in Pebble Beach is 138 from the regular tees, and, thus, the challenges will be significant. Theoretically, the higher the slope rating, the more difficult the course, and the more likely you will need a tourniquet.

At Brookside, the Local Rules are posted in the locker room and pro shop but do not appear on the scorecard. By taking a few moments to review these amendments to the standard Rules of Golf, you will be prepared for unforeseen circumstances and also understand the advantages the Local Rules may provide.

While you're checking the scorecard, talk to a member, a regular, or the local pro about the course. Good questions to ask relate to wind conditions, major characteristics or features, quality of conditioning, toughest holes, types of grasses, speed of the greens, height of the rough, and overall strategy.

It is also helpful to know who designed the course, and, if it's someone familiar, refresh your memory regarding his concepts and tendencies. If the designer has written a course description and it is available, read it. For example, newcomers playing my Spanish Trail Golf and Country Club course in Las Vegas would benefit from my capsule evaluation: "This is a big, strong course with large, undulating greens, reflecting the nearby mountains and surrounding desert. However, if you attack the targets too aggressively, you will be faced with difficult recovery shots around the greens."

How to Use a Yardage Book

Yardage books have long been a staple of the PGA Tour and may someday become a standard part of the average player's course-analysis kit. I've included an illustration and photograph of the 390-yard par-4 first hole at Medinah Country Club near Chicago from "The Book" prepared by George Lucas for the 1990 U.S. Open. A quick look reveals the level of detail available to pros during a tournament round.

Because this book was created for pros, all yardages are from the championship tees. Major features (trees, slopes, bunkers, water, etc.) are marked, and distances from the tee are noted. Yardage

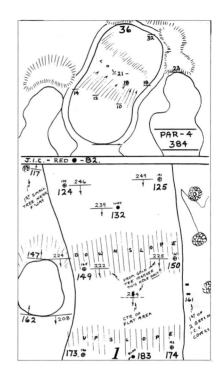

YARDAGE BOOKS, SUCH AS "THE BOOK" BY GEORGE LUCAS, ARE HELPFUL IN DETERMINING DISTANCES TO VARIOUS FEATURES ON HOLES LIKE THE PAR-4 FIRST AT MEDINAH COUNTRY CLUB IN ILLINOIS.

Always look for slope within the teeing area, as it can affect the flight of your shot.

books show slopes and exact measurements to the best landing areas. The movement of the fairway also is clearly indicated.

A yardage book gives the tour pros an edge against the course. Until such books become available to all golfers, you must learn to do some of this observation and homework for yourself. I recommend you make a book for your home course. You can do this at a time when your course is empty, or you can do it progressively during playing rounds. Jot down distances, elevations, features — any data that helps you understand the design strategy of each hole. You'll be amazed by how much more precisely you will look at your course and how much better you will play it.

KEY FACTORS AFFECTING TEE PLAY

Whatever type of tee style or situation you encounter, take a few moments to study the key factors — elevation, location, and slope — which directly affect your tee shot. This approach will improve your chances of starting well on a hole.

Elevation off the tee has two important consequences. First, when a tee is positioned well above the fairway, your actual landing area becomes more difficult to determine, due to the increased distance you will obtain from the vertical drop. Second, the preferred landing area is tighter because an errant shot will travel farther through the air and therefore farther off line before encountering a land form. Thus, the greater the tee's elevation, the more you should move toward selecting your straightest club.

A good elevation example can be found on the 212-yard par-3 eighth hole at our Chateau Whistler course in British Columbia. You stand 80 feet above the green, which is flanked by a lake on the left and a large rock formation on the right. Any shot that curves to the left results in a lost ball, and shots that wander to the right sometimes carom off the solid granite face. Occasionally, a lucky bounce will wind up on the green. Most times, though, you'll need the Canadian Mounties to find the ball.

On other occasions we have reversed the situation and placed the tee below the elevation of the landing area. This technique was used at the 413-yard par-4 eighteenth hole at University Ridge near Madison, Wisconsin. The rise in elevation from tee to fairway helps control errant shots because it stops the ball quickly. In tee situations of this type, you should focus on trajectory and maximum carry. Psychologically, many players feel awkward and uncomfortable with the landing area above them and overswing. On some occasions, a 3-wood is a better choice than a driver because the additional loft will help you get the ball airborne.

Another important consideration is tee location in relation to other features. A good example is a tee tucked into areas protected by trees, bushes, rocks, or even edges of mountains. On such protected tees, you are placed in a controlled environment that affords little information about the prevailing wind conditions. Always check to see if there is a difference between wind conditions on a sheltered tee and the rest of the hole. Conversely, the

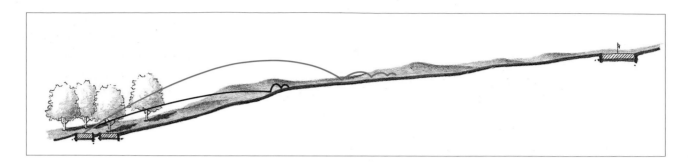

The par-4 eighteenth hole at University Ridge Golf Course rises dramatically from the tee to the landing area, making trajectory a prime consideration in your club selection.

designer may position a tee so that it is exposed to wind and weather in an attempt to distract you and cause uncertainty.

As a general rule, most tee sites are chosen with some psychological element in mind. For example, some tees are positioned to require a forced carry, thereby creating a certain intimidation factor for the golfer. Often such shots appear more difficult than they actually are. Designers love to employ this technique to create indecisiveness about your club and shot selection.

Next, there is slope within the teeing area itself. Frequently, tees are tipped slightly to create drainage, and, occasionally, this slope will affect playing values. For example, a tee that is tipped from back to front can cause you to hit a lower shot than you intended. Combine this effect with an uphill hole like University Ridge's eighteenth and you'll lose a lot of distance. You should check the pitch of each tee by standing slightly back and to its side.

Most designers will tip the tee in the direction of the proper shot. Sometimes, however, the terrain forces the designer to tilt the tee against the natural path of the hole to create surface drainage. For example, the proper shot is right to left, but the tee tilts left to right. Such a situation calls for additional adjustment on your part. Be aware of this possibility.

At Weston Hills Country Club's par-4 ninth hole in Fort Lauderdale, Florida, identifying major and secondary features can help you select your best route to the green.

HELPFUL THINGS YOU CAN DO ON ANY TEE

Once you arrive at the tee, identify the hole's major features. Usually, there is something substantial (natural or artificial) designed into the hole, like a stream running down the left side, a large tree set in the middle of the fairway, a line of bunkers on the right, a contoured fairway, a lake in front of the green, or a slope on a putting surface. Isolate a key feature on every hole. By so doing, a basic strategy for attacking the hole should come into focus.

Also try to make mental notes of secondary features. For example: Where has the designer marked the "edges" of the hole? Where does short rough end and tall rough begin? Is there a tree line edging the rough? Does the hole fall off into a ravine or water hazard? How does the skyline define a hole? What effect is the wind having on this shot? Are there out-of-bounds areas to contend with, and where are the markers? How do the playing conditions affect bounce or roll?

Taking all these factors into account, you must now face the most important question in terms of playing decisions — how much risk are you willing to take? This process entails weighing the rewards of a well-executed stroke versus the consequences of a misplayed shot. A number of considerations must be evaluated and factored into your decision making, including the penalties you may suffer, your ensuing options, your ability to recover from trouble — and how well you are hitting the ball. If you're having trouble making solid contact, don't get greedy. Once you have assessed the benefits and liabilities of the preferred landing area, your target should become apparent.

On some holes, the options are clear. For instance, if you're standing on appropriately named Waterloo, the 576-yard par-5 thirteenth at The Dunes and Beach Club in Myrtle Beach, South Carolina, a lake hugs the entire right side, threatening anyone who slices and daring the accurate and longer players to take shortcuts. You can be heroic and hang it out over the alligators or play conservatively, possibly saving a ball.

On other holes, the choices are less obvious. The 531-yard par-5 third hole at the Windsor Club in Vero Beach, Florida, is straight forward and straight away. Trees and dense brush flank both sides of the hole, and three fairway bunkers on the left tell you where to aim your tee shot: stay clear of the sand and favor the right side of the fairway. While most golfers perceive doglegs or bending holes to be the toughest tee shots to execute, I believe straight holes are more difficult because there is only one option. If you don't hit the ball straight, you're doomed.

No matter what type of hole, most tee shots have some gambling element. It may be as simple as aiming toward a hazard to get a

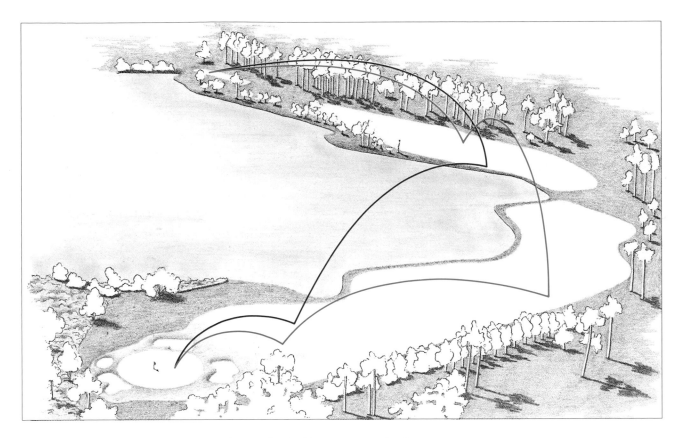

better second shot or as bold as flying the ball over a stand of
trees to cut off part of the hole.

In the chesslike game you're playing, early hazards are meant to win
the hole immediately for the designer. To defeat him, it is critical
to understand his intent and decide on the best way to counter.
For example, the driver often is not the best club to use in a gambling situation. Frequently, the architect relies on the golfer's
temptation and greed to overcome the proper decision not to use
a driver. On many par-4s and -5s, the smart play is a fairway
wood or a long iron.

Next, try to find the perfect route to the hole. To quote fellow
designer Jack Nicklaus, "There is an ideal route for every golf hole

*The par-5 thirteenth at the Dunes
and Beach Club in Myrtle Beach, South
Carolina, offers various attack options.*

ever built. The more precisely you can identify it, the greater your chances for success."

One good way to identify the ideal route is to observe the position of the pin and work backward to the tee with your eyes. The pin position will dictate the best angle of approach from the fairway and thus the prime landing area for your tee shot. The ideal route can change daily according to different pin and tee locations, weather considerations, and other playing conditions.

Another useful technique for determining the optimum route is to analyze the green area and its features. Their location and shape frequently will indicate a primary green entrance, similar to the way in which a pin suggests a specific strategy by its location. For example, the front right portion of a green may be guarded by water, thus making the extreme left side of the fairway the perfect spot from which to attack the target.

If you can't see either the pin or the green from the tee, look at the movement of the hole. Oftentimes the hole's shape will show you the best position from which to approach the final target. For example, if the hole doglegs from right to left, the left side of the landing area will usually offer the preferred angle of approach and will shorten the overall distance to be covered.

You should also consider your dominant playing characteristics. Do you hook or slice? Can you work the ball in a controlled fashion from left or right? You want to use your natural shot-making pattern to your advantage and play the hole's layout with your strengths.

Now, realistically decide on the number of shots you'll need to reach the green, which may be different from "regulation" shots as defined by par. It's your number that counts. If it's a long par-5 and you need five shots to get home, then plan for five. If you can quickly organize these shots into a connected series, it will help you estimate distances and decide what clubs you'll need. By sticking to your game plan as closely as possible, you will save yourself unnecessary strokes and frustration.

Finally, look for a major marker that will guide your tee shot. It can be a tree, a distant point on the horizon, a hazard, or some other marker. Most regulars at a course have figured out these markers. However, use them only if they fit into your distance and shot plan. For example, on the 560-yard par-5 eighteenth hole at Penha Longa Golf Club near Lisbon, Portugal, the ideal tee shot is struck directly toward a white tower that looms behind the green.

Always pick a specific target area in which to land your ball. LPGA golfer Martha Nause once told me, "We played a course in Canada where the fairways were 70 yards wide and I had a terrible time. I never picked a target area off the tee and I was in trouble all day long. I just said, 'Hit it anywhere,' and anywhere was inevitably a fairway bunker."

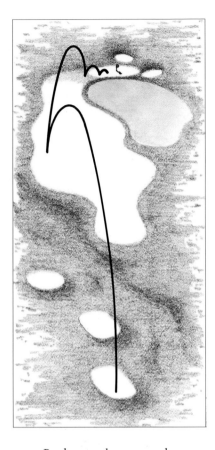

By observing the green complex and its surrounding features on holes like the par-4 ninth at Spanish Trail Golf and Country Club's Sunrise Nine in Las Vegas, Nevada, the optimum route becomes obvious.

Where you land is normally more important than the length of your tee shot. Position usually takes precedence over distance. Getting a good lie and angle for the next shot is paramount, and success off the tee almost guarantees that you'll be in good position through the entire hole. Failing to do so will cause headaches, sore backs, and double-bogeys.

BALL-TEEING TECHNIQUES

Before teeing off, several important decisions should be considered. First, which tee will you play? Each set produces what we call courses-within-a-course, that is, a variety of lengths and strategic angles on a single hole.

Next, walk around the tee. Go to the back and sight the green; then move forward. Most important, walk from one side of the tee to the other and see how your perspective changes. Now stand between the tee markers and determine your landing area. Getting into the habit of using this technique will reveal hidden landing areas and alternate routes to your target.

A well-known example of this technique occurred during the 1979 U.S. Open at Inverness Golf Club in Toledo, Ohio. During a practice round, veteran pro Lon Hinkle discovered a small opening in the trees down the left-hand side of the dogleg par-5 eighth hole. Standing on the back of the tee, Hinkle realized that if he positioned himself in the back left corner of the tee and aimed left, he could play down the adjacent seventeenth fairway and cut approximately 60 yards off the hole, reducing it from 528 yards to about 470. This distance reduction enabled him to reach the green with a mid-iron. Overnight, distraught USGA officials, less than thrilled with Hinkle's creativity, blocked his route by planting a 24-foot spruce tree.

The illustration showing our 538-yard par-5 seventeenth hole at Pine Lake Golf Club in Hyōgo Prefecture, Japan, demonstrates

THE TOWER BEHIND THE GREEN AT PENHA LONGA GOLF CLUB'S PAR-5 EIGHTEENTH HOLE IN PORTUGAL IS AN EXCELLENT TARGET FOR THE TEE SHOT.

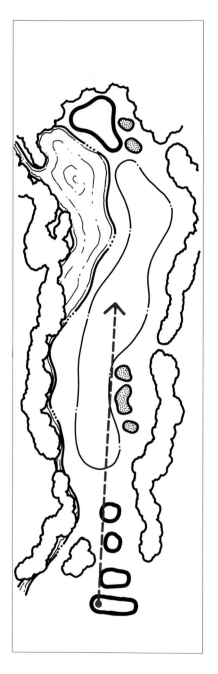

If you move to the far left side of the teeing area on the par-5 seventeenth hole at Pine Lake Golf Club in Japan, it will improve your view of the landing area.

how observing the landing area from the extreme left portion of the teeing area lets you see more of the hole. A large bunker protects the right side of the fairway, but the prime landing area is just beyond the bunker. This optimum target is obvious to players teeing off from the left side, but unclear to those who hit from the right or middle part of the tee.

Spend a few moments checking the alignment of the tee markers. Don't assume that they are pointed along your intended line. Also check to see if the tee lines up with the fairway itself. You may get properly aligned with the tee and find that you are hitting diagonally across the fairway. All tees are not necessarily aimed toward the ideal target area. Small tees (particularly on steep terrain) are shaped and aligned to the existing topography. It is always the golfer's task to determine the correct line of play.

The Rules allow you to tee up anywhere between the markers and no more than two club lengths behind them. You do not have to stand within the tee markers, but the ball must be between them, and never in front of them. In most cases, one side of the tee will offer a preferred angle of attack to your target. As a rule of thumb, skilled players will usually place the ball on the side of the tee that contains the greatest trouble and play away from that trouble toward the safer or open side of the hole.

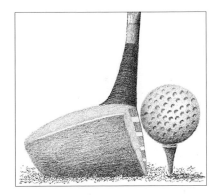

Always use a wooden tee because it provides a perfect lie. It may look good to throw a ball down and casually hit it, but in tournament play you'll almost never see a pro do this except right after making a triple-bogey. On very rare occasions, however, an experienced player will set the ball on the grass in order to combat the effects of a strong headwind. Even in this situation, however, the ball is placed meticulously on a "raised area" constructed out of the turf, which is permissible within the Rules of Golf. The Rules also allow you to alter other portions of the teeing surface before you play your shot, such as moving loose impediments, stepping behind your ball to flatten the ground, or extracting weeds and grass from the soil.

How high you tee a ball relates directly to the club and shot you've chosen. The driver is teed higher to match the ascending blow you want. Middle or short irons should be teed lower to get the most out of the descending blow you want for these clubs. When playing into the wind, tee the ball lower or plan on bringing a baseball glove or butterfly net to catch your pop-ups.

One last tip. It is common to talk about "going to school" on someone else's putt, but you can also do this with drives, especially on par-3 holes where you can observe club selection, distance, and how the ball reacts when it hits the green. You'll also gain a more precise feeling for the pin placement. The Rules, however, prohibit you from asking your opponent's advice. With holes other than par-3s, check to see how the fairway reacts, which features come into play, and how wind affects the ball.

A driver is usually teed slightly higher to catch the ball on the upswing, while irons should be teed progressively lower to facilitate a descending blow.

Every tee is a clean start and an opportunity for you to maximize your chances of ending up in the fairway. Remember, the key to good scoring is finding the fairway off the tee.

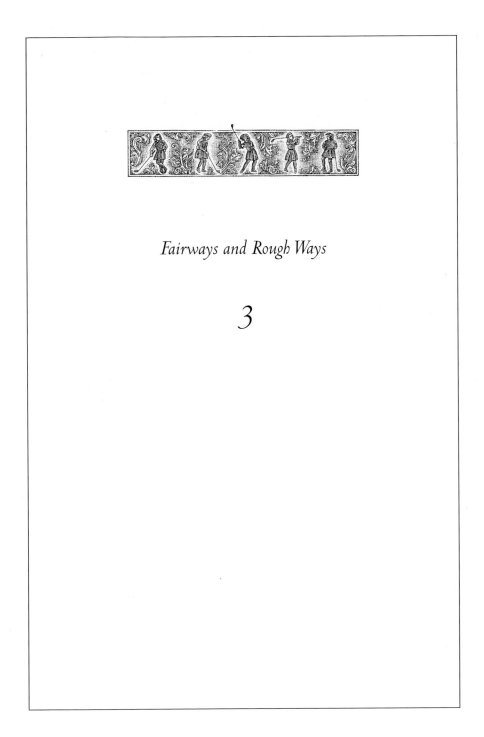

Fairways and Rough Ways

3

THE TENTH FAIRWAY AT WEDGEWOOD GOLF AND COUNTRY
CLUB IN COLUMBUS, OHIO, INCORPORATES TREES, BUNKERS,
AND ROUGH, MAKING SHOT SELECTION A CHALLENGE.

PRECEDING PAGE:
TILTED FAIRWAYS, LIKE THE PAR-4 THIRD HOLE AT
CHATEAU WHISTLER GOLF RESORT IN BRITISH COLUMBIA, CANADA,
PRESENT SIDEHILL LIE AND STANCE CONSIDERATIONS.

The word "fairway" sends positive vibrations down the spine of every golfer. It suggests nicely clipped turf with the ball sitting up. Landing on it confirms that you're on track, playing the hole the way the designer laid it out. To stay in the fairway during an entire round is an incredible achievement for any golfer.

The PGA Tour keeps weekly statistics for fairway accuracy, and Calvin Peete made a habit of collecting the year-end bonus awarded to the leader. Peete, a short hitter by tour standards, led this category for ten consecutive years (1981–1990) and won eleven tour events during that period. Obviously, it pays to stay on the short grass.

Another good example of the importance of being on the fairway was provided by professional David Graham. Trailing tournament leader George Burns by three strokes starting the last round of the 1981 U.S. Open, Graham shot a brilliant 67 that earned him the victory. Most amazing was Graham's remarkable performance of hitting every fairway except for the first on that final day at the Merion Golf Club in Ardmore, Pennsylvania, thereby avoiding the thick and treacherous U.S. Open rough.

Ways to Look at a Fairway

Conceptually, the fairway is much more than short grass. I see a fairway as the keystone that connects all critical components of a hole. Trees, rough, bunkers, water, and the green's position are all tied to the fairway in deliberate fashion.

If you study the photo of our 415-yard par-4 tenth hole at Wedgewood Golf and Country Club in Columbus, Ohio, you will see how its individual elements dovetail. In the first landing area, the fairway shaping incorporates a stand of trees down the left side, which serves as a natural defense; the bunker on the

Following Page:
At Ruuhikoski Golf Course
in Finland, a carefully conceived route
plan utilized the natural flow of the
landscape and the existing features on site.

right is positioned next to thick rough and signals trouble ahead. From that point on, the fairway contours connect all other features for the remainder of the hole, namely, the greenside bunkers, the putting surface, and the surrounding trees.

When laying out a course, we first develop a route plan for all eighteen holes. We look for the natural flow of the land in arranging the sequence of holes. Each hole is carefully marked with a centerline, that is, a straight line from the tee to a "turnpoint" in the fairway and then to the green. The fairway then becomes a path, the main link between tee and green.

The routing for our Ruuhikoski Golf Club near Seinäjoki, Finland, required careful study of a complex site just south of the Arctic Circle. The land consisted of wild, frozen tundra and boggy, claylike soil, presenting tremendous drainage problems. It also was necessary to contend with cumbersome rock outcroppings and fast-rushing streams interspersed with trees. After two days of walking, looking, and probing shot making, a route plan began to materialize in my mind. The winding river became the spine of the concept, and the incorporation of the rocks and trees into the design resulted in what is now a fine course stretching 6,800 yards.

By mentally drawing a centerline for each fairway, you will find its natural path, and you'll develop a true feeling for how a hole functions directionally. As a result, you will be able to work your ball along the line of the hole. The more you go with the flow of a hole, the better off you are. Don't spend a round fighting the natural path of the golf course.

Too often a golfer standing on a tee or fairway only asks, Where should I aim? Equally important questions are How does the fairway expand and contract? and How does it turn and angle? Focusing on the widening and narrowing of a fairway often unlocks the designer's plan because it reveals where he thinks

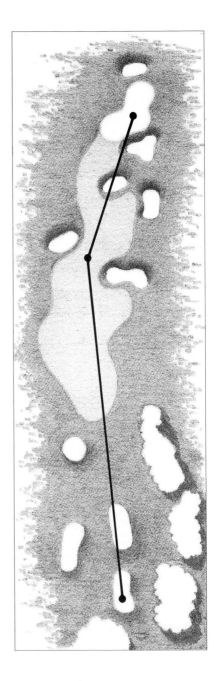

The par-4 fifteenth hole at Club de Bonmont Terres Noves near Reus, Spain, shows how the fairway narrows, placing a premium on accuracy for long hitters.

On the par-4 first hole at Silverado Country Club's North Course in Napa, California, the flattish fairway provides the golfer with a level lie from which to attack the hole.

different players will land the ball. A simple defense is to tighten the fairway at various points with rough, a tree, a bunker, a slope, or other feature. Whenever you can, take a moment to estimate fairway widths or even pace them off. Once you have completed this analytical process, you can then intelligently make your decision about where to aim.

In the construction bid documents submitted for our courses, we include the following language: "The contractor's task is to shape and contour the fairways, as directed by the Designer, taking into account the importance of golf playing values and fine aesthetic appearance. The Designer reserves the right to alter the design or shape of any fairway where such alteration is in the best interests of the total golf course design. The Designer has the right to have fairways reworked as often as necessary in order to obtain the desired artistic and playing characteristics."

This contractual provision emphasizes how important the configuration and contouring of a fairway are to creating a good golf hole. To give you a better understanding of these concepts, I will tell you how I go about fairway design.

Remember that a designer can set up a fairway in ways that are virtually limitless. To help you go beyond the basic fairway elements explained above, I will discuss below some common fairway shapes and styles. Note, however, that very often the designer uses combinations of shapes and styles on a single hole.

When I speak of a fairway's shape, I am referring to its three-dimensional or topographical characteristics. For example, a fairway can be flat, tilted, or a combination of both these shapes. On the other hand, a fairway's style describes its two-dimensional configurations — as we see them, for example, on a route plan. A dogleg is one common style.

FAIRWAY SHAPES

Flat or Baseline Fairways

When I say "baseline golf," I am referring to situations where the topography is dead flat prior to design. Such was the case for the Palo Alto Municipal Golf Course in Palo Alto, California, and portions of the Silverado Country Club in Napa, California. Prior to modern earth-moving techniques, fairways generally consisted of level, flat playing surfaces. Many earlier American golf courses, especially those built during the depression or after World War II until the late 1960s, feature nearly level, straightforward fairways. In the last twenty to twenty-five years, designers have advanced the art of creating elevation changes to improve both playing values and surface drainage.

Where feasible, the designer will integrate trees, mounds, and water hazards to give otherwise bland areas greater definition and

visual contrast. Make sure you evaluate the benefits and liabilities
of these features when selecting your shots.

Mounded Fairways

Early courses were built on dune land sprinkled with natural
mounds and hollows, which the holes meandered around, over, and
through. As golf course design evolved, mounding became a
distinctive feature of many holes. The celebrated Donald Ross was
noted for his contouring of mounds around greens and aprons.
Ross's mounds contained varying amounts of slope, which produced
a variety of lies, stances, and shot-making requirements.

Today, mounds are often created to replicate the traditional look
of many Old World courses. Heavy earth-moving equipment
is used, with the goal of making the mounds appear as natural as
possible. On occasion, larger mounds can be overdone, sometimes to the point of absurdity, which can result in awkward lies.

Designers employ mounds to perform a wide variety of functions. Fairway mounds may be deployed like bunkers as a defense. As physical obstructions, mounds can kill an otherwise promising drive, deflect the ball into trouble, or leave you with a difficult downhill, sidehill, or uphill lie. As visual obstructions, they can block your view of the target and create uncertainty. Situated in front of a green, they require a deft pitch to clear them and stop the ball quickly. Mounds can also act as markers off the tee or as indicators of the friendly and forbidding sides of the fairway. Ask yourself these questions when dealing with fairway mounds: Do they tell me where to hit, or are they primarily aesthetic? Are they hiding a potential landing area? How severe are they in terms of deflection and playability?

Rolling Fairways

Some of our courses — such as Chenal in Arkansas, Highland Springs in Missouri, University Ridge at Madison, and Crystal Tree near Chicago — share a common ground in the following sense: they are all built on moderately rolling terrain. Designers consider such property ideal because it offers natural contours and slopes that keep the golfer guessing but aren't as severe as those found on steeper sites.

From a topographical viewpoint, rolling terrain affords ups and downs, much like moguls on a ski run. It allows a designer to create, if he chooses, many undulations, from swales to plateaus. When playing a rolling course, you should pay particular attention to the amount of roll you will get on each shot because that distance may spell the difference between hitting off a flat or uphill lie instead of a trickier downslope.

Whenever you are on a slope, try standing to the side of your ball and learn to gauge the angle of the rise. The land becomes part of your loft and distance equation. Draw an imaginary line off the angle of the ground to see how much it adds to the trajectory of

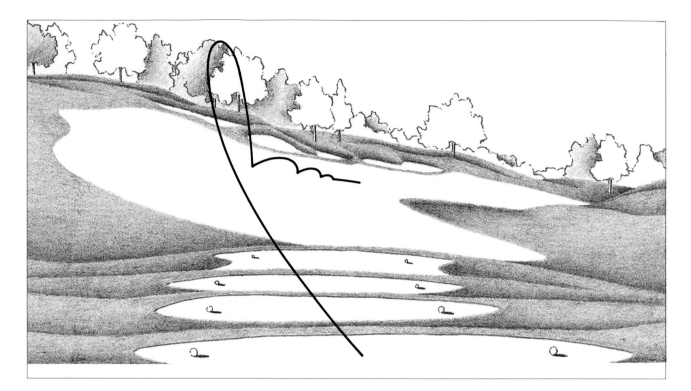

your intended shot. Careful evaluation of a slope can significantly increase your chances of selecting the proper club and shot.

Tilted Fairways

Here I am referring to fairways (or sections of a fairway) that cant sideways with some degree of sharpness. When confronted with tilted (banked) fairways, remember our pool comparison. In this situation you will have to estimate how much angle will be added to your shot after it hits the slope. It is critical to take this into consideration, because on a severe slope the wrong bounce can send you off the fairway into serious trouble.

Now that you have a better understanding of the different ways in which designers shape a fairway to obtain desired playing values, let's look at some basic fairway styles and the way they affect your shot-making decisions.

Linear

Linear fairways are one of the most common styles a golfer faces. Here the fairway flows in a straight line between tee and green and often provides you with a clear view of the entire hole. Although at first glance it may appear that a shot down the middle of the fairway would be ideal, the important point to grasp is that one side of the fairway generally offers a preferred angle of attack to your target depending on pin position and hazard location.

Consider the 436-yard par-4 first hole at Silverado Country Club's North Course, illustrated earlier in this chapter. Standing on the tee you have an unobstructed view of the pin. It is the kind of hole you should mentally play backward because the pin location dictates which side of the fairway provides the best angle of approach. If the pin is positioned to the right behind the large bunker, the left side of the fairway is a far superior place from which to attack. If the pin is located on the left side of the green, the right side will afford you the best opportunity for success.

Doglegged

The earliest courses generally ran along the margin of the sea, with relatively straight sightlines from tee to green. As courses moved inland and trees became part of the strategic challenge, designers bent holes to hide the final target. Thus, the dogleg was born. On average, you can expect to see at least three or four pronounced dogleg holes in a round.

For instance, our 380-yard par-4 thirteenth hole at Jefferson Golf and Country Club in Columbus, Ohio, doglegs sharply to the right. This medium-length hole, although appearing relatively tame on the scorecard, is strengthened considerably by the fairway's configuration. The dogleg creates uncertainty about the amount

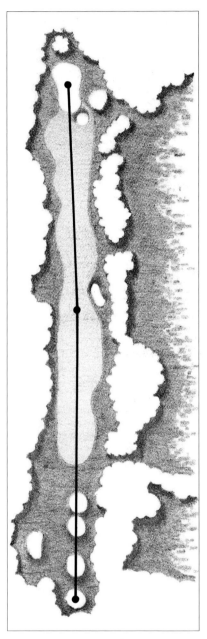

On linear fairways, like the par-4 thirteenth hole at Miho Country Club in Japan, the pin location and green defenses determine the preferred landing area in the fairway.

of landing area off the tee, because you can't see either it or the preferred route to the green, which is also hidden.

Occasionally on a par-5 hole you will encounter a double dogleg. The accompanying illustration is the 492-yard par-5 thirteenth hole at Golf and Country Club de Bossey in Haute Savoie, France, on the Swiss border, which shows the variety of angle challenges a player must solve on double doglegs. Note how the fairway bends in two different directions. Holes of this nature require careful planning because most golfers need at least two shots to set up their approach to the green. Even if you hit an accurate tee shot, you aren't off the hook. Oftentimes the second shot is even more challenging to ensure favorable positioning for your approach.

Here are four basic questions to ask about any dogleg: (1) What line should I take to shorten the hole? (2) Is cutting the dogleg worth the risk? (3) How much landing area do I have beyond the corner of the dogleg? (4) Can I hit through the dogleg?

Corridored

As golf course development moved inland to parkland and mountain areas, designers began to encounter sites that were heavily forested throughout. Routing a course in a sylvan setting constitutes a genuine dilemma for the designer. On one hand, correctly laid out fairways can be imbued with startling natural beauty and golfing definition. On the other hand, poorly routed courses that fail to incorporate sound golf and environmental concepts will be disasters.

Thick stands of trees require a meticulous and painstaking effort to route a high-quality course while preserving and, perhaps, enhancing the site's natural assets. Mandatory understanding of the topography is gained only by spending endless hours walking and plotting the ground under the tree canopy. Aerial photos

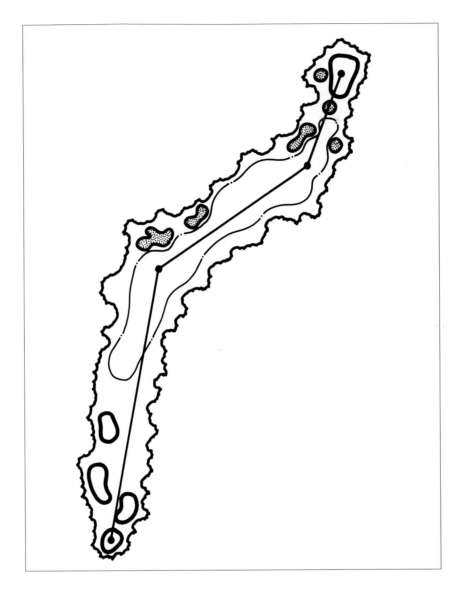

Thoughtful planning is a must on
double-doglegs, such as the par-5 thirteenth
at Golf and Country Club de Bossey in
France, where the fairway bends in two directions.

FOLLOWING PAGE:

THE TREES ON THE PAR-4 TENTH HOLE AT SUGARLOAF
GOLF CLUB IN CARRABASSETT VALLEY, MAINE, ACT AS A NATURAL
DEFENSE AND SHOULD BE AVOIDED AT ALL COSTS.

and observations from elevated areas can be poor indicators of the topography under the trees.

After the topography has been carefully plotted, a route plan is prepared and the centerlines (narrow paths allowing sight and walking access) are cut through the trees to verify that the routing works from a golfing point of view. Great efforts are made at early stages to identify trees to be preserved by incorporation into the course. Last, full-scale tree clearing is carried out to create tree-lined fairways, commonly called "corridored fairways."

Note the accompanying photo of the 335-yard par-4 tenth hole at my Sugarloaf Golf Club in Carrabassett, Maine. The corridored fairway was literally carved out of thick forest. The trees act as a perceptual guide for the golfer and also serve as a natural defense against shots that are misdirected or poorly struck. Designers view these heavily treed areas as major obstacles, and you should take all appropriate measures to avoid the woods, whether hitting to a corridored fairway or off one.

Split

Split fairways can be created by separating their sections horizontally by inserting a hazard between them or vertically by an elevation change. Because their playing considerations are similar, I will discuss both types at this point.

The first type splits the fairway into two sections on the same horizontal plane. These sections are usually divided by bunkers, rough, or, on rare occasions, a small water hazard. One fairway segment offers a superior position from which to attack the hole, but reaching it involves greater risk than shooting to the safer landing area. The other portion is less risky but results in a longer or more difficult route to the final target. The area that separates the two fairways generally penalizes you in some way, with the severity depending on the type and design of the hazard utilized.

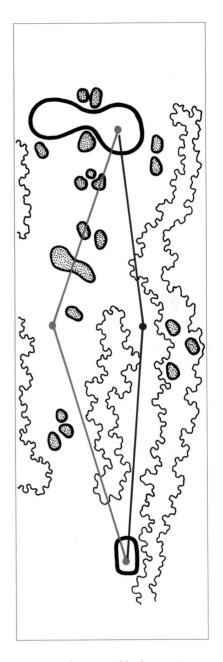

A split fairway like the par-4 fourth hole at St. Andrews usually offers one risky route that pays dividends for golfers who execute properly.

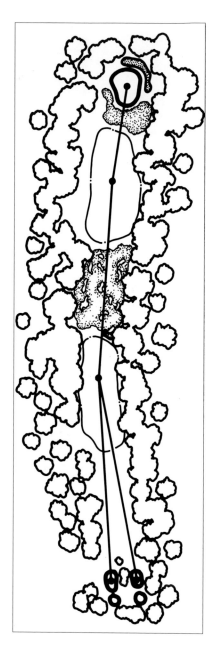

*The key to finding island fairways,
like the par-5 seventh at Pine Valley Golf
Club in Clementon, New Jersey,
is accuracy and restraint.*

The second type is a fairway split vertically into two (or more) elevations, with or without hazards or obstacles dividing it. The elevations generally are tied together by severe slopes, causing most shots to finish in a reasonably level area. This fairway design is much more forgiving than the first type because there is a larger total landing area. However, one side has a better angle of attack to the target.

Several examples of split fairways are the 463-yard par-4 fourth hole at St. Andrews, the 557-yard par-5 ninth hole at Poppy Hills, and the 363-yard par-4 sixth hole at Makena Resort's Mountain Course in Maui, Hawaii. As the illustrations in this chapter show, split fairways can be created in various ways.

Split fairways are another good example of the risk-reward philosophy of design. In every case, the designer is saying, "Think a minute about which route you want to take. One will give you a definite advantage on this hole." He is also trying to make you waver between the two, so be decisive.

Island

Some of the world's most celebrated island fairways are found at Pine Valley in Clementon, New Jersey. More than half the holes at Pine Valley require hopscotch-like playing from tee to fairway. The illustration shows the 585-yard par-5 seventh hole, which may be the epitome of island fairway play.

Island fairways pose three basic challenges: (I) Hitting them is more a matter of direction than distance. Island fairways usually have severe penalties on their perimeters, meaning that errant shots often wind up in hazards. (2) They require restraint in order to hit the ball a certain distance. Trouble always lurks beyond the prime landing area, so be sure you know the distance to the farthest edge and choose your club accordingly. (3) If you

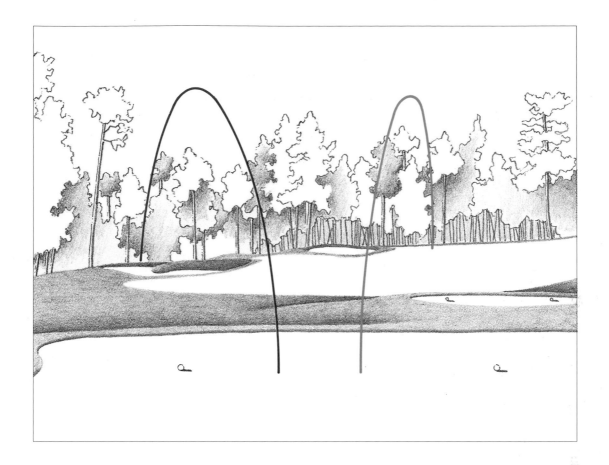

When confronted by split fairways, like the par-5
ninth hole at Poppy Hills Golf Course in Pebble Beach,
California, choose a target based on your ability.

On the par-4 seventeenth hole at Edinburgh USA
Golf Course in Brooklyn Park, Minnesota, an
island fairway is surrounded by water.

don't carry the obstacle in front of you, you will inevitably suffer its penalties.

Because a course's grass substantially affects how it plays, it will be instructive for us to focus, at this point, on the playing characteristics of some common grasses. First, designers select grasses that will thrive in the course's particular environment. At Spanish Bay, in Pebble Beach, California, we had a seaside links setting, so we specified fescue — a hardy, tawny, drought-resistant grass usually associated with Scottish links courses. An additional benefit derived from this specification was that the fescue grass helped keep water usage to a minimum at Spanish Bay during the drought that began shortly after it opened. For a traditional northern course or locales with cool to moderate temperatures, we normally select bentgrass. In mountain settings, ryegrass oftentimes is the choice. In southern climates, hardy bermudagrass fits the bill. Most important, remember that the type of grass substantially affects how a course plays.

What do you need to know about various golf course grasses to play better? You should be able to recognize the common varieties of grass and know two of their important playing characteristics, specifically the fairway lies each generally produces and the challenges they pose when used in the rough.

Let's take a look at the various types of grasses you are likely to encounter on golf courses throughout the world. From a shotmaking viewpoint, the most important thing to know is how each grass type affects your lie and the action of the clubhead on the ball. Below I've given you a thumbnail guide for each grass, from physical appearance to climatic factors and playing characteristics.

Bentgrass: This is a cool-season grass with a fine leaf-blade texture that is used predominantly for fairways. Bentgrass thrives in the northeastern, northwestern and western United States, Canada, and certain areas of Europe and Japan. It cannot tolerate a combination of heat and humidity, and it requires steady irrigation. As a fairway surface, bentgrass produces a tight lie. Shots played off bentgrass fairways usually travel shorter distances because of this tight lie. Except for rare occasions, bentgrass is not used in rough areas because its fine-bladed qualities are best kept at low heights.

Bermudagrass (called kuchgrass in some areas): A warm-season grass with fine (hybrid bermuda) to broad, coarse (common bermuda) leaf blades, depending on the type utilized, bermudagrass is used in both fairways and rough areas, and is commonly found in the southern United States, the Caribbean, and other tropical climates. It grows well in hot and humid conditions, thrives on less water than bentgrass, and has vigorous growth characteristics. When maintained at fairway height, bermudagrass allows the ball to sit up well and provides little clubhead resistance. Bermuda divots disintegrate, but the grass regenerates quickly. When maintained at rough heights, bermuda is stiff and wiry and will grab or twist a clubhead.

Bluegrass: This is a cool-season grass with longer, moderate-size leaf blades and clubhead resistance properties somewhere between those of bentgrass and those of bermudagrass. It thrives in a variety of regions and is able to withstand substantial temperature changes. Bluegrass is sometimes used simultaneously in fairways and rough areas, but in most cases today it is used in the rough to provide a brilliant color contrast to bentgrass fairways. It can be an attractive grass choice in mountain and prairie settings. On a bluegrass fairway, shots will travel distances similar to shots on bentgrass fairways. Escape from bluegrass rough can be difficult, especially if its blades are allowed to grow long.

Fescue: This cool-season grass possesses a fine to coarse leaf-blade texture and is known for thriving by the sea. It is prevalent in

AT KATSURA GOLF COURSE'S PAR-4 TWELFTH HOLE IN JAPAN, CONTRASTING GRASS VARIETIES ARE USED TO DISTINGUISH FAIRWAY AND ROUGH.

the British Isles and is often associated with links courses. There are two basic types: fine fescue, which is the thinner version, and tall or wild fescue, which has thick, coarse leaf blades. Fine fescue produces light clubhead resistance and, when used as a rough grass, is easier to escape from than other cool-season grasses such as bluegrass or ryegrass. On the other hand, tall or wild fescue is becoming increasingly popular as a rough grass and, on occasion, is maintained to produce a dramatic visual contrast with fairways. When tall fescue is blended with a bluegrass-rye mixture in the rough, escape becomes a chore because of the tangly, swirly nature of the grasses. As a fairway surface, fine fescue, like bentgrass, provides firm, tight lies, causing shots to travel shortened distances.

Kikuyugrass: Thriving in mild climates, this all-season grass has thick, wiry blades and a rapid growth pattern. It can spread quickly, invading other areas of the course. On a fairway of properly maintained kikuyu, shots will travel distances similar to those achieved on bentgrass or fescue. As a rough grass, kikuyu's strong, wiry texture will grab your clubhead, as well as abruptly stop a ball landing in it. If kikuyu is left unmaintained, escape becomes almost impossible.

Annual Bluegrass (generally known as poa annua or poa): This seasonal grass thrives under moist conditions. It usually makes its presence known in the spring when it invades portions of the golf course planted with bentgrass or fescue. Poa has a sticky, clumpy, irregular quality in both fairways and rough areas, and its effect is exacerbated by its growth rate, which far outstrips that of fescue or bentgrass. Agronomists studying the properties of poa annua conclude that it has a photosynthetic rate 40 percent faster than bentgrass, thus producing patchy, nonuniform fairways and rough areas during its seasonal life cycle. Its qualities can make poa difficult to play from, especially from the collars and in the rough near the green.

Knowing the basic grass types and their playing characteristics is essential for improved scoring.

BENTGRASS

BERMUDAGRASS

FINE FESCUE

POA ANNUA

RYEGRASS

ZOYSIAGRASS

Ryegrass: This cool-season grass thrives under most conditions except intense heat and humidity. Its playing characteristics and resistance properties closely resemble those of bluegrass. Because ryegrass establishes itself quickly, it is frequently used to overseed bermudagrass fairways and rough areas in the winter months. As a fairway surface, ryegrass produces a lush, healthy growth of turf grass in a short period of time. It holds moisture well. Escape from ryegrass rough can be difficult due to moderate clubhead resistance.

Zoysia: A warm-season grass with a coarse leaf-blade texture, zoysia grows well in warmer climates. It can handle the extreme temperature changes of the transition zone in the United States and provides a fairway lie similar to that of bermudagrass, with the ball sitting up and the grass itself causing little resistance. Because of zoysia's healthy growth habit and slight clubhead resistance, shots tend to travel substantial distances. In Japan, a form of zoysia known as korai is used on the fairways, and another variety called noshiba is used in the rough areas. Noshiba is considered to be more escapable than bermudagrass.

Substantial research is now under way to develop new varieties of turf grass that will require less water, fertilizer, and pest-control chemicals. Improved strains of buffalograss, paspalum, poa, and other grasses likely will be found on future courses.

LIES AND HOW TO PLAY THEM

Lies can be analyzed in two basic ways: first, by reference to the slope where the ball stops, and second, by the way the ball rests in the grass. Understanding the playing effect of each of these parameters will enable you to select the best shot-making approach.

Naturally, one reason designers give contours to fairways is to test your shot-selection and shot-making skills. While we offer level landing areas to afford golfers the opportunity to position themselves with a level lie, we know that many times your ball will come to rest in places that will require you to adjust your stance and swing. They embrace the classic four "unlevel" lies — uphill, downhill, sidehill (ball below feet) from right to left, and sidehill (ball above feet) from left to right.

Three points to remember: (1) don't become flustered by an unlevel lie; (2) always note the direction and amount of slope in the lie before you set up; and (3) make adjustments for a particular lie with the specific purpose of creating a level swing plane.

Pay particular attention to direction. Downhill shots tend to go right, and your shot will fly lower and longer. In distance terms, this means you will probably want to use less club. On uphill shots, the ball tends to squirt left and balloon into the air. The uphill angle adds loft to your distance equation, so expect shots to fly higher and shorter.

On sidehill shots where the ball is above your feet, the degree of slope will flatten your swing, producing a hook. The sharper the slope, the flatter your swing, and the more the ball will go left, so aim right. The opposite applies when the ball is below your feet.

Now let's look at what fairway and rough grasses do to your shot.

Ball on Fairway

Note what kind of grass you're on (you usually need to do this only once, at the beginning of a round) and mentally review its playing characteristics. Do not overlook the fact, however, that many courses have two or more types of grass. For instance, at Menlo Country Club near my home in Woodside, California, many fairways have three or four types of grass. Be prepared to adjust to the variety of shot-making challenges that these situations present.

When the ball is above your feet, shots will tend to hook.
When the ball is below your feet, shots will tend to slice.
When faced with an uphill lie, the ball will fly higher and shorter.
When confronted with a downhill lie, the ball will fly lower and longer.

Here are some basic reminders for fairway play. When your ball is resting on the fairway, the cool-climate grasses generally have the following playing characteristics: the ball sits close to the ground and will travel shorter distances because greater contact with the soil causes more clubhead resistance. This is commonly referred to as a "tight" or "thin" lie.

Conversely, the warm-climate grasses generally have these playing characteristics: on the fairway the ball sits up well, and you will experience little clubhead resistance; the ball carries farther in these conditions.

Occasionally, designers build "bowls" into fairways, to make them more receptive. The 621-yard par-5 seventh hole at the Makena Resort's Ocean Course is a good example, and you'll find lots of divots in the approach area. A divot lie is never as bad as it seems. Generally, it will be a tight lie, the ball won't go as far, and it will spin more because of the lack of turf. For best results, remember to strike the ball with a sharply descending blow.

Ball in Rough

In relation to fairways, designers use rough in two ways. First, in open areas where there is little definition in the way of natural features, we use rough to define a hole and as a defense against errant or misguided shots. Whether it is tall natural grass growing along the fairway or the fearsome "secondary" U.S. Open cut of four to five inches, tournament committees and superintendents can make rough so punishing that it takes other defending features out of play and becomes a golfer's major worry. Happily, this happens only on a limited basis. However, tall grass is still one of the surest ways to make a golfer pay for errant tee shots. Therefore, try to follow Calvin Peete's example and stay on the fairway.

Second, designers also use rough as a protective buffer or saving device. Rough can be high and thick enough to keep your ball

When playing from a tight
lie, strike the ball with a descending
blow and take a little extra club.

from encountering even worse trouble. For example, we may leave
a healthy cut of rough along the edge of a lake, stream, or
bunker to save a ball from such hazards.

The 545-yard par-5 fifth hole at the Springfield Golf Club in
Nagoya, Japan, has a large lake that guards the right side of the
hole. This hazard is bordered by a 5- to 7-yard-wide patch of
rough that will slow shots hit through the fairway, often saving
the golfer's ball from a watery grave.

Sometimes, designers orchestrate grasses in ways you might not
expect. For example, we may choose different grasses for fairway
and rough. The subtle color variance more clearly defines the
shape of the hole and can help your perception. Be alert for
situations where you may encounter two different grasses with
distinct playing characteristics on the same hole.

At Brookside Country Club our grass selection was important
for the overall success of the course. Faced with an open, treeless

site devoid of other natural features and vegetation, I knew that visual contrast would play aesthetic and strategic roles. Consequently, we delineated fairways and rough areas with grasses of different colors and textures. We used a mix of bent and ryegrass for the fairways and a blend of rye and tall fescue grass in the rough. The contrast was striking. This "visual roadmap" offers the observant golfer a clear path to the hole.

Understanding the way the rough has been cut is vital to escaping from it. One trick is to look for cutting patterns left by the mower. On most courses, the rough is mowed in straight-line swaths running from tee to green. Depending on where the maintenance crew begins its mowing, the direction in which the grass lies will have a dramatic effect on how far you are able to advance the ball. For example, if the first cut of rough is mowed from green to tee, the grass will lie against you. Conversely, if the grass is mowed from tee to green, it will lie toward the green and escape will be easier.

Be ready for the classic "flier" lie. Simply explained, a flier lie exists when at impact a small amount of grass gets caught between the ball and the clubface, with two consequences: (1) it shuts the clubface slightly, reducing loft on your club and thus increasing distance; and (2) the grooves on your clubface will not be able to impart spin to the ball, causing you to lose distance control. Result: your ball comes out of rough grass lower and hotter and usually rolls farther. A variation of the flier lie occurs when at impact water is between the ball and clubface. The results are similar. Be alert for this situation if the grass is wet as the result of rain, early morning dew, or irrigation.

Facing a flier lie, you definitely want more loft on your club, which means you'll hit a shorter club to compensate for the increased distance a flier produces. One of the best methods for combating this lie is to open your clubface slightly, because the rough will grab the clubface and close it. Make sure to apply a sharply descend-

Flier lies, where grass gets between
the ball and clubface, result in increased
distance and lack of control.

ing blow to the ball, and be sure to factor in the extra distance you're likely to attain.

If at impact there is a substantial amount of grass between the clubface and the ball, you will have the opposite effect of a flier lie because the ball will travel a much shorter than normal distance. With a heavy lie be realistic about how far you can hit the shot. If the grass is four to six inches high, you will encounter heavy resistance. Favor a high-lofted club and don't get greedy for distance. The key is to advance the ball back into the fairway.

Other Off-Fairway Challenges

While playing our Desert Dunes course in Desert Hot Springs, California, one day, I was standing at the edge of a fairway and heard one of my design colleagues speaking but could barely see him among the mesquite scrub, sagebrush, and other vegetation bordering the hole. He'd hit a winger sideways, and after a few minutes, I said, "C'mon, let's go. That one's lost." After a moment of painful silence, he replied, "The ball's not the only thing lost. I can't find my way out of here!"

Sometimes rough areas take on a different look from just turf grass or trees, as the above story illustrates. Rough can be the desert in its natural state or the rocky terrain near a mountainside. When we built Desert Dunes, the client wanted to keep development costs and environmental disturbance to a minimum. Our solution was to contour only the turfed areas and wind them in and around the natural desert landscape. The result is a series of fairways bordered by native desert. The premium here is on accuracy because the area off the fairway is virtually unplayable, unless you like picking thorns out of your trousers.

THE ROUGH AREAS ON DESERT COURSES, LIKE THE PAR-3 FIFTH AT DESERT DUNES IN DESERT HOT SPRINGS, CALIFORNIA, FREQUENTLY RESULT IN UNPLAYABLE LIES AND THORNY PREDICAMENTS.

Here are some useful points to remember as you advance toward the hole from fairway or rough. First, identify the challenges in your next target zone. What are the major and minor obstacles, and where are the alternative landing areas? Second, check your lie and factor in other conditions that will affect your shot. Is it a clean or grassy lie? What type of grass is it? In what direction does the slope or hillside run?

Third, formulate or reformulate a strategy for finishing the hole. Look at your next shot as it relates either to reaching the green or to setting up the following shot. Fourth, pick a specific target, whether it be an area of the fairway, a portion of the green, or the flagstick. Your purpose is to create a positive mental picture for your swing. Finally, between strokes, always observe what lies ahead — elevation changes, the bend in a fairway, a green slope, or a pin position.

FINAL FAIRWAY TIPS

Get a sneak preview of coming holes. All good players take the opportunity to observe upcoming holes before they play them. Usually, you will be able to look at the hole from a vantage point totally different from the one you will have while actually playing it. This technique allows you to experience one of the perspectives the designer had when creating it, which may help you develop a plan for playing the hole by understanding how it was laid out.

When the shots aren't working and there are too many of them, remember that the most important shot in golf is the next shot, and don't get down on yourself. I think this applies most often on the fairway, because we tend to "lose it" more often somewhere between tee and green. Work hard to block out the last shot when it is unsuccessful and refocus on your plan for the hole.

It is also important to realize that while the fairway is the preferred position, it is not the only way to reach the green. When the first two shepherds competed, one took the obvious route along the grass while the other found the dunes more direct but more difficult. In those days, they weren't obsessed with perfect lies or avoiding the tall natural grasses that grew along the links. Just making solid contact was their primary goal, and they figured they could hit the ball from any lie and succeed just as well.

As a player, you should visualize all parts of the golf course as an opportunity to complete the hole in the fewest number of strokes. Granted, the fairway is usually the optimum route to your final target, but many other areas of the course that contain rough, trees, and friendly hazards can offer a useful path to the hole if you understand their playing characteristics.

A great example of this occurred during the final round of the 1991 Masters at Augusta. On the 420-yard par-4 uphill dogleg eighteenth hole, Ian Woosnam of Wales was nursing a one-stroke advantage. Knowing that a par was all that stood between him and victory, the long-hitting Woosnam took the dangerous left-side fairway bunker out of play by powering his drive into grassy hollows beyond the bunker and left of it in what used to be a practice area. Woosnam had a wide-open approach shot, reached the green, and two-putted for a winning par.

Let's face another fact: you simply aren't going to hit every fairway. Even Calvin Peete misses a few. The key is learning how to improvise when you find yourself off the fairway, whether in rough, a difficult lie, or a bunker. Bunkers give most golfers fits, but experts frequently consider them a godsend. In the next chapter, I'll explain why.

Bunkers

4

THE "CHURCH PEWS" BUNKER ON THE PAR-4 THIRD
HOLE AT OAKMONT COUNTRY CLUB IN PENNSYLVANIA HAS A
PENAL CHARACTER, MAKING ESCAPE EXTREMELY DIFFICULT.

PRECEDING PAGE:
THE PAR-5 TWELFTH HOLE AT WESTON
HILLS FEATURES A CLUSTER BUNKERING PATTERN
ON THE INSIDE OF THE DOGLEG.

102

 From simple holes in the ground to carefully angled and sculpted shields protecting the green, bunkers have become a standard part of the designer's defense arsenal.

On the Old Course at St. Andrews, one of the world's most famous bunkers is found, the Road Hole bunker. For countless years it has claimed the balls, rounds, and even the golfing careers of players sentenced to its torments. In the 1978 British Open, Tommy Nakajima of Japan was challenging for the lead when he accidentally putted into this cavernous bunker, which protects the back-left pin placement he was confronting. Nakajima made a nine and disappeared from contention.

Across the sea in the New World, at Oakmont Country Club in Pennsylvania, you'll find the Church Pews, an ironic moniker for one of the world's most satanic bunkers. Standing guard on the left side of the landing area off the third tee, it is deep, broad, and treacherous, with two-foot trenches.

While the Road Hole and the Church Pews bunkers have been the stages for notorious golfing calamities, the average player finds a bunker at the local public golf course to be almost as threatening. Touring professional Gary Player believes that "fear of sand" is at the root of most golfers' problems.

Player, one of the world's best bunker players, strongly supports the notion that amateurs almost universally live in terror of hitting out of sand. Most golfers view sand as some slippery and disastrous substance that keeps them off balance and interferes with their attempts to hit a normal golf shot.

Contrary to the instincts of many golfers, all sand is not to be feared. Indeed, in some situations the sand may be "friendly" to the point that you may actually want to be in it. Conversely, some types of bunkers are so penal that your top priority should be avoiding

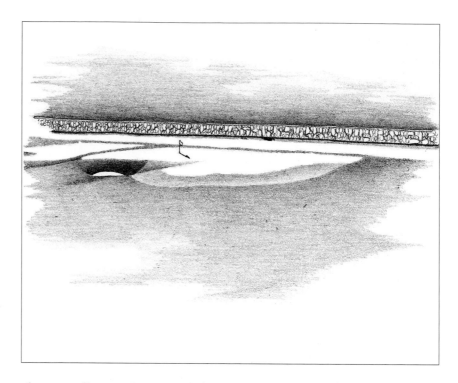

*The Road Hole at St. Andrews contains
a deep pot bunker that defends a substantial
portion of the putting surface.*

them at all costs. Your attitude toward the sand feature confronting
you should be determined solely by its characteristics and functions — which I will analyze in this chapter.

Given these realities, I have to state the obvious: if you can learn
how to play a bunker shot like the pros — not nearly as farfetched
an idea as you think — you won't flinch when you wind up in a
relatively benign sand feature. Most expert players prefer gentle
bunkers to rough because they can control the ball more easily and
thus have a better chance to save par. For them, the toughest part
is raking the sand.

Don't hesitate to take a lesson on bunker play. It will take practice
to master the sand, but imagine the difference in your game if you
had the same confidence standing over most bunker shots as you
do with a good lie on a fairway. With a little knowledge, technique,
and change in your psychological outlook, you'll be amazed how
fast you can improve.

Because sand was indigenous to the early courses, every designer has found a way to incorporate it in one form or another. Sand is used in many ways — for aesthetic contrast with the green land-scape, as a buffer between holes, and as a shot-making challenge. The bunker is the most common form of hazard.

Initially, bunkers were located helter-skelter around the course and were mostly just hollows and pockets that had been formed over time by sheep trying to keep warm from the wind. Early designers simply adjusted the teeing areas and fairways to fit the natural bunker pattern. Not until the game spread to England were bunkers created as part of the strategy during the routing of a course to penalize missed shots. This design philosophy resulted in courses being built with as many as 150 to 200 bunkers to make sure there was plenty of trouble.

The Great Depression put an end to that because courses couldn't afford to maintain hordes of bunkers. It was Bobby Jones, Alister Mackenzie, and my father who espoused the philosophy that bunkers should be located beyond the beginning golfer's reach but in play for the intermediate or expert player alike from their respective tees. In other words, bunkers should be strategically placed in relation to a hole's multiple teeing areas.

The key to proper bunkering often is not how many but where they are positioned. More doesn't always produce a higher degree of difficulty. Often, one thoughtfully placed bunker in a prime landing or approach area is all that is required to challenge most golfers, upset their rhythm, or, sometimes, help them visualize the proper way to attack a hole.

Statistically speaking, the average golf course contains between 80 and 100 bunkers. Many great courses, however, are not within this range. Augusta National originally had only 26 and now has 40; Pine Valley uses long, sandy waste areas (which technically are not bunkers but possess many of their characteristics and playing values); Oakmont, with 187 bunkers, is close to some of the British courses. Oakland Hills has 118; Baltusrol 115; Merion 113; Winged Foot 76; and Medinah 55.

The Olympic Club in San Francisco, site of the 1955, 1966, and 1987 U.S. Open, has only one fairway bunker — at the 437-yard par-4 sixth hole. The reason is simple: the long, narrow, tree-lined course, often damp from fog and moisture, is plenty tough without them. Moreover, the bunker on the left side of the sixth hole actually saves a player from a worse fate, as the fairway at that point drops sharply to the left into thick pine trees.

On my own courses, I have no preconceived number in mind but do believe that bunkers should be used selectively and be balanced with other challenges.

Let me briefly explain how designers deploy and build bunkers. After we finalize a routing plan, we sketch in preliminary bunker positions. Once fairway paths are cleared and earth-moving operations completed, we rough-shape each bunker with a bulldozer to see how our original placements work on the "as-built" holes. We then make adjustments based on length of the hole, flow of fairways, and wind considerations. In some instances, this process reveals that a bunker does not work as originally anticipated, and we may actually remove bunkers entirely and relocate them somewhere else. At this point, we are beginning to "tie in" bunkers with other parts of the hole.

After we feel comfortable with the positioning, we do the final shaping. Sometimes we place white sheets in the bunkers to test their visual qualities; we may stand on a truck or bulldozer to see how they look from a distance. We also hit golf balls to understand exactly how they catch various types of shots. If we're satisfied, we grass their edges and slopes, sod them if necessary, cut the final shape, and add sand to make the finished bunkers you have to contend with.

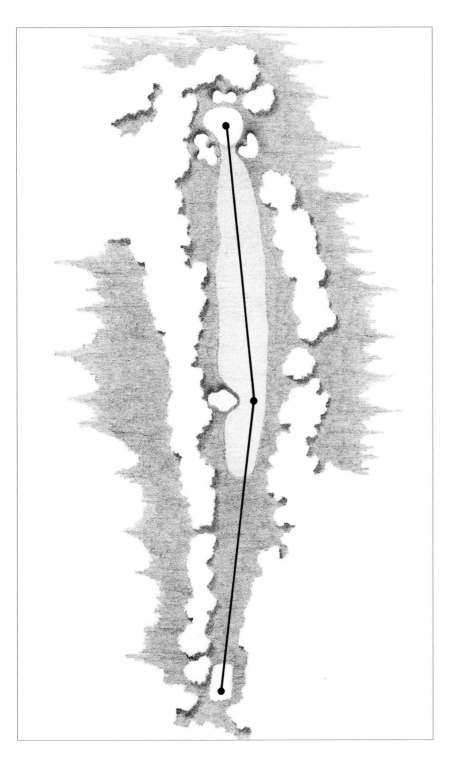

With large rows of tall trees lining virtually every hole, the Olympic Club in San Francisco, California, site of three U.S. Open Championships, has only one fairway bunker.

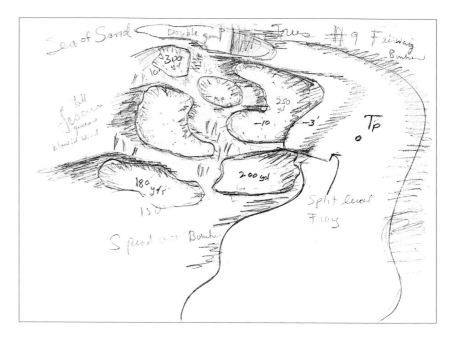

Now, let's look at bunkers to decide where they fall on the spectrum between "friendly" bunkers that you may prefer to be in given the nature of adjacent terrain and "penal" bunkers that you want to avoid at all costs. During this analysis, we will look at bunkers both as individual types and as components of "bunkering patterns."

BUNKER TYPES

In alphabetical order, here are eight types of bunkers and their playing characteristics. Note that the same bunker is sometimes called by two or three different names — excluding expletives.

Carry Bunker: This normally flat or low-lying bunker partially protrudes out into the fairway, allowing golfers to play directly over it. Although a carry bunker may look intimidating, it almost always is positioned well short of the preferred landing area and is easily flown. Even if you find yourself in one, escape is relatively easy due to the flat, inviting lies you usually receive in them. Once you decide you are confronting a carry bunker, don't psych yourself

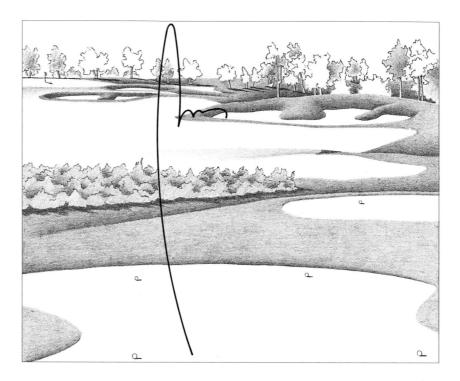

out worrying about this sand feature. Oftentimes, this kind of bunker will be found on the inside of a dogleg hole.

Collection Bunker: Also known as a "bathtub" or "gathering" bunker, this type derives its character from the ground surrounding it, which is sculpted to channel the ball into the bunker. A collection bunker can be very deep, as exemplified by the walk-in style bunker that is similar to a military bunker — deep and big enough to hold a squad of soldiers. This type of bunker usually deploys a high front wall, which often forces you to play backward or sideways to recover. Most are found on older courses, with a few examples in the United States, such as those in the driving areas at the 477-yard par-5 tenth hole at Cypress Point in Pebble Beach, California, and the 412-yard par-4 tenth hole at our Weston Hills course in Fort Lauderdale, Florida.

Collection bunkers generally are fairly penal, and you should strive to steer clear of them. Again, it is critical for you to decide what type of bunker you are encountering in order to decisively plan your shot. Should you fail to make this analysis, you will be courting disaster. If you find yourself in a collection bunker, play the simplest shot available to get out. Advancing the ball toward the hole is of secondary importance.

Definition Bunker: Designers usually employ this type of bunker to highlight a target zone — the landing area off the tee, the second-shot landing zone on a par-5, or the green itself. The definition bunker's severity can vary widely. Escape from a deep bunker with a sharp face is much tougher than play from a shallow bunker, and, generally, the degree of difficulty built into the bunker relates to the length and type of shot required and its position in relation to the fairway. The definition bunker is the type you will encounter most frequently.

A definition bunker can also help you judge the distance of your approach shots into the green, especially elevated shots. In these instances, the bunker provides you with depth perception. The rule is to study the flagstick to see how much of it is visible. If you can see most of the pin, you know it's fairly close to the bunker. If you can't, the pin is likely to be positioned farther back on the green, so adjust your shot selection for this additional distance.

A good example is found on the 110-yard par-3 fifth hole at our Sun Valley, Idaho, course. Bunkering at the front and back of the green not only provides depth perception but also frames the target, allowing distance to be judged more accurately. During the Danny Thompson Memorial Tournament, an annual charity event held there, I found out how helpful such bunkers can be. While playing with baseball great Vernon Law, I aimed over the front bunkers and made a hole in one.

Directional or Target Bunker: Many well-designed holes use a bunker to reveal a shot-making line or direction. Sometimes I'll include what seems to be a meaningless fairway bunker — out beyond the

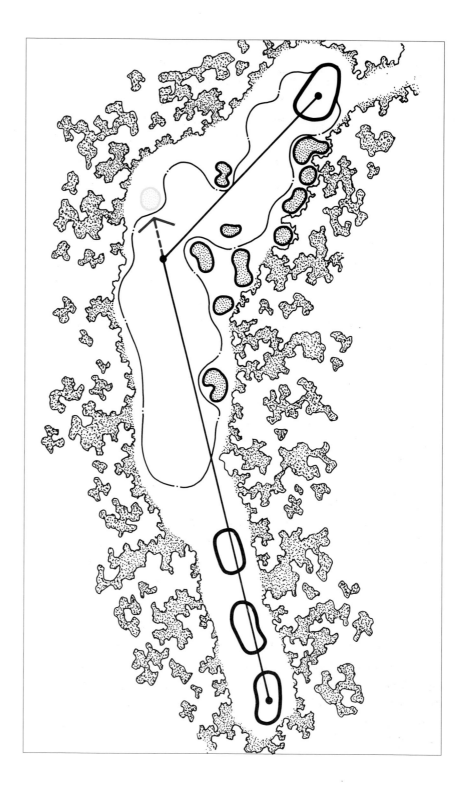

*The par-4 sixth hole at Spanish Bay
has a target bunker, which can be useful
for proper alignment from the tee.*

reach of all but the longest hitters — to act as an aiming reference. This technique is commonly employed on dogleg holes to give golfers a greater feel for how the hole flows.

Take the 395-yard par-4 sixth hole at Spanish Bay. The target bunker on the left side of the hole is not in play even for the big hitters (except in windy conditions). Later, at the 394-yard par-4 ninth, the left-hand bunker pattern from tee to green is quite important because it defines the hole and orients your tee shot.

Face Bunker: Invariably a part of a green complex, this bunker shows its "face" to the approaching golfer. Strategically, it can be used for deception, to conceal a green's true distance. Its penal quality varies according to the severity of the face's incline. The steeper the slope, the more difficult the bunker. A face bunker with any downslope in its front portion makes for difficult and sometimes impossible shots.

Pot Bunker: This small, round-shaped bunker, generally with steep sides, makes recovery difficult because of the need for a severely elevated shot and the cramped space in which you must set yourself. The pot bunker is quite common on older links courses and is appearing more frequently on newer U.S. courses where today's designers are creating enhancements of this type, particularly in terms of size and depth. One of the most famous pot bunkers in the world guards the front edge of the tenth green at Pine Valley. This bunker is so steep and deep that, for many golfers, escape may require several swings, taking an unplayable lie, or even a hand mashie.

Saving Bunker: Designed to spare you a far worse fate, this bunker can save the day. For example, at the 520-yard par-5 fourteenth hole at Mission Viejo Country Club in Mission Viejo, California, my father and I used saving bunkers to prevent a slightly mishit shot from rolling down a steep hill. Believe it or not, designers aren't total sadists in our use of bunkers — sometimes we actually try to help you!

Frequently, a saving bunker will be placed next to a sharp slope, water, the out-of-bounds, or behind a green that has trouble beyond its back edge. For instance, on the 242-yard par-3 third hole at Squaw Creek Resort near Lake Tahoe, California, the left edge of the putting surface has a bunker adjacent to it that saves shots from rolling down a steep incline into some pine trees or the out-of-bounds. Look for saving bunkers placed adjacent to highly penal areas, and soon you'll see that the designer is saying, "Stay away from this spot because trouble awaits." Also, you should recognize here that the sand is much more friendly than the alternative — and factor this knowledge into your shot selection.

In like manner, if the green is elevated with a severe sideslope running away, a bunker may be placed in front or on the edge to keep the ball from rolling all the way back to the bottom of the hill should you mishit or misclub and land short. For example, the eighteenth green at Lansdowne Golf Resort near Washington, D.C., has a friendly bunker on the right side that saves you from going down into a valley. On such a hole, if you're a good sand player and the pin is located near the bunker, you may want to be aggressive and aim for that portion of the green because recovery from an uphill bunker lie is relatively easy. Again, by understanding the design's risks and rewards, you will be able to adapt the situation to your game.

Waste Bunker: The long, mostly flat, low-maintenance waste bunker is often characterized by a firm texture and native vegetation flanking or surrounding it. Waste bunkers can often run 50 or more yards in length and protect a large portion of fairway. Occasionally, they contain small islands in their central areas or peninsulas of land that jut out sporadically, creating some unusual lies. In most cases, the sand is compacted and, if properly maintained, provides good opportunities for escape. If you land in a waste bunker, don't panic. The key here is to pick the ball cleanly off the sand for full shots, and, on shorter shots, consider chipping the

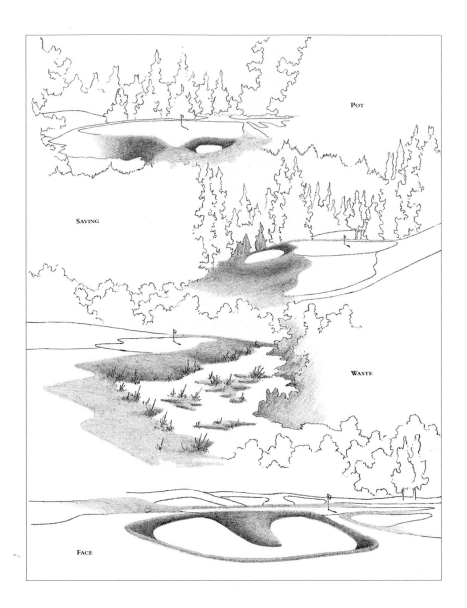

POT

SAVING

WASTE

FACE

*Pot, saving, waste, and face bunkers have
different playing characteristics, and understanding these
distinctions is essential for proper shot selection.*

115

ball rather than blasting it. Waste bunkers can also parallel major trouble and thus save you from a worse fate.

Not to be confused with the waste bunker but closely related are what designers term "waste areas." They feature combinations of sand, native grasses, natural vegetation, and, occasionally, other indigenous plants. Waste areas technically are not hazards, but they can be effectively utilized to defend many portions of the golf course, from crossing a fairway to skirting the entire length of a hole. Requiring little or no maintenance, they often produce odd and difficult lies in the tradition of the early links game. Because of the uncertainties created by these areas, recovery play can involve various unknown challenges, and you should approach waste areas with extreme caution. In this venue, the old adage really holds true — "when in doubt, wedge it out."

Some illustrative waste areas are the sandy waste areas at Colt and Crump's masterpiece Pine Valley; the transition waste areas at Pete Dye's South Carolina Kiawah Island Resort, where the 1991 Ryder Cup Matches were held; the dunescape on the first five holes at my father's Spyglass Hill Golf Course; and the tawny-colored waste areas we created at The Windsor Club.

More and more, today's designers are incorporating grass swales and hollows into their courses. They aren't as visible as sand and often result in awkward stances and lies. While a grass bunker or swale may appear less intimidating than a sand bunker, it can actually be much more penal, especially for expert players, because the grass is generally maintained at rough height and control of the ball is much more demanding. Therefore, just because no sand bunkers appear on a hole, do not assume you are home free. Be especially careful to look for these less obvious but potentially even more pernicious areas.

BUNKERING PATTERNS ARE PREVALENT AT SPANISH BAY'S PAR-5 FOUR-TEENTH HOLE, FORCING GOLFERS TO MAKE CLEAR-CUT DECISIONS OR PAY THE PRICE.

The early theory of placing bunkers saw them as "walls" that bluntly blocked a golfer's advance to the green. Over time they became a series of carefully arranged "traps" aimed at catching inaccurate or weakly hit shots. The positioning of hazards has been influenced by three factors: the increasing length today's players exhibit; the desire of good designers to set up a course that tests expert, intermediate, and beginning golfers; and the improved visual effects that a properly located and designed bunker can bring to the playing experience.

When contemplating the various concepts designers use to challenge you, start by analyzing the general placement of bunkers on a course. Often this approach can help you formulate a strategy that will work over an entire round. At Spanish Bay, for example, we built a links course in the Scottish tradition. Ten holes have only a single bunker near the green, which is in direct contrast to modern green defense theory, where a series of bunkers encourages golfers to fly their shots directly onto the green. At Spanish Bay, we planned firm to hard greens so that airborne shots would not necessarily stay on the putting surfaces. We then opened up the entrances to invite the run-up shot, but also deployed hollows and other challenges that require the golfer to bounce the ball into the target from the proper angle in order to succeed.

Spanish Bay, however, has numerous bunkering patterns in and along the fairway landing areas. To wit, Spanish Bay uses central bunkering patterns on four holes, cluster bunkering patterns on seven holes, and framing bunkers on more than half the holes. Therefore, what appears at first glance to be a fairly open course takes on the personality of a narrow, precise golfing challenge as a result of the many different bunkering types and patterns.

Next, I will analyze six common bunkering patterns you will encounter. Although they are related to the bunker types discussed above, in developing strategy you should regard them as distinct hazards that affect your shot-making choices.

Central Bunkering: A central bunkering pattern divides a fairway into two sections, providing you with two or more playing options for a given landing area. This pattern can be located in any landing area, but in most cases look for it in the tee-shot landing area or the second landing area on a par-5. Bunkers tend to be long and thin, or of the pot style, allowing enough room for two sections of fairway to flank them. The 377-yard par-4 eighteenth hole at Windsor Club has a central bunkering pattern off the tee. When you are confronted with such a challenge, choose a specific route, because indecision almost invariably leads to a difficult approach shot from a bunker.

Cluster Bunkering: The cluster bunkering concept makes use of a grouping of three or more bunkers to add definition and visual contrast to an otherwise bland or open hole site. This pattern usually has directional ramifications, telling you to steer clear of it and where to find the best route to the hole.

On the 524-yard par-5 second hole at Poipu Bay Golf Resort on the island of Kauai, Hawaii, you will find a stringlike cluster of bunkers stretching from the green's front right edge parallel to the fairway and for a distance of about 90 yards. Among other consequences, this bunkering pattern eliminates any inclination you might have of taking a shortcut to the right as a means of reaching the green more easily.

Another challenging cluster bunkering pattern awaits players who tackle the 533-yard par-5 sixteenth hole at University Ridge, which is reachable in two for long hitters. The intention was to break up a

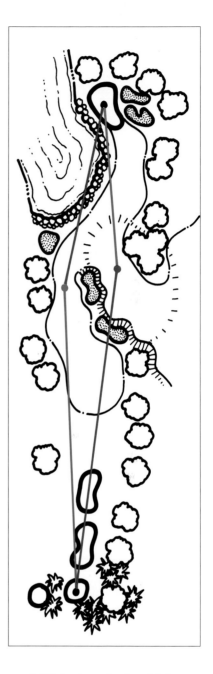

At Windsor's par-4 eighteenth hole, a central bunkering pattern creates distinct teeing options for players in the landing area.

*Cluster bunkering, such as this group on
the par-5 second hole at Poipu Bay Resort,
provides a warning signal to golfers.*

WEDGEWOOD'S PAR-4 THIRTEENTH HOLE CONTAINS A
SERIES OF SHARPLY ANGLED CROSS BUNKERS THAT PRESENT BOTH
DISTANCE AND DIRECTIONAL CONSIDERATIONS FOR PLAYERS.

section of open farmland into a well-defined second landing area near a boomerang-shaped green. The cluster pattern in front of the putting surface forces you to either carry the second shot to the green's right side or play to the fairway area on the left side of the hole. Getting caught by this pattern will drive both your score and temperature up quickly.

Cross Patterns: This series of bunkers off the tee is usually set at a diagonal, bisecting the width of the fairway. I like to angle them sharply, thereby creating a more complicated distance versus direction analysis. The more yardage you cut off, the greater the risk you will not carry the bunkers. A good example is the 415-yard par-4 thirteenth at Wedgewood, shown in this chapter. A series of three bunkers was laid out in diagonal fashion, forcing players to consider both distance and direction simultaneously. Entering one of these bunkers makes for a tough recovery.

Occasionally, a cross bunkering pattern will cut directly across the fairway with little or no angle. This occurs on the 623-yard par-5 seventeenth hole at the Baltusrol Country Club's lower course, site of many U.S. Open Championships. In this scenario, the distance factor becomes more relevant than direction, so concentrate on selecting a club and a shot that will allow you to carry these obstacles comfortably.

Framing or Bracket Patterns: Arranged in pairs or a series of pairs on opposite sides of the fairway or green, bracket bunkers squeeze the fairway landing area and green entrances, challenging players to hit the ball between or over them. They also force you to plan exactly how you should place your tee shot or what angle you want for an approach. Once positioned about 200 yards off the tee, bracket bunkers now are more likely to be found farther out in the pro's driving area (240 to 270 yards off the tee) to penalize inaccuracy. Sometimes, on a long par-4 or par-5, you will find two sets of bracket bunkers to test short and long hitters.

My father liked to "frame greens" with this bunkering pattern to help define their location and thus help players to visually determine where the edges of the putting surface began. More important, bracket bunkers near greens serve to produce pin locations of varying degrees of difficulty. Generally, pin positions near the center of the green will be easier, and flagsticks placed near the edges will be tougher to attack. This factor gives tournament officials and superintendents the opportunity to fine-tune the setup of the golf course to achieve appropriate levels of playing challenge for any competition.

A good example of this technique is found at my father's Firestone Country Club in Akron, Ohio, where bracket bunkering can challenge the world-class players who participate in the World Series of Golf, or where the pins can be located in an easier spot for regular membership play. By carefully evaluating the location of

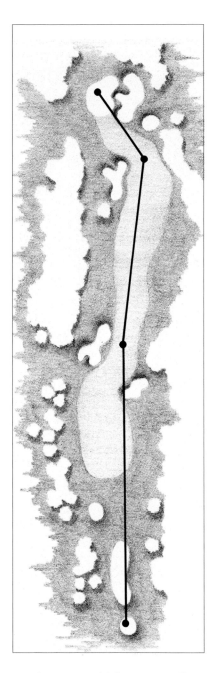

The par-5 fourth hole at Poppy Hills features a staggered bunkering pattern that tests players of all abilities.

The short par-3 tenth hole at Chateau Whistler is surrounded by bunkers, making aerial approach mandatory.

the pin in relation to the bracket bunkers, you can determine the correct approach angle to a green and the proper shot required.

Staggered Patterns: This variation of the bracket pattern (used by architects such as Mackenzie and Tillinghast) involves placing bunkers at different distances on opposite sides of the fairway, rather than in balanced pairs. This arrangement causes golfers to ponder which bunker will have the greater effect on their shots. Similar to the way in which a set of modern tees defends against players of varying lengths and skill levels, the staggered bunkering pattern is used to ensure that players consider accuracy rather than pure distance as a means to defeat a hole. A good example is the 560-yard par-5 fourth at Poppy Hills, shown in the accompanying illustration.

When properly implemented, this concept will oftentimes turn a simple fairway surface into a snaking type of fairway and require golfers to evaluate carefully which portion of the landing area should become their target. Although you might expect to see this type of pattern mainly in landing areas off the tee, it is also commonly used near your final target.

The 450-yard par-4 seventeenth hole at Highland Springs in Springfield, Missouri, is a strong hole where bunkering patterns and the movement of the fairway tell you to stay left. There are two reachable bunkers on the right side of the fairway and an unreachable bunker down the left side. If you do your homework, you'll discover that the left bunker is the ideal target and is not in play even for long hitters.

Surrounding Pattern: This bunkering pattern is reserved exclusively for green surfaces on those occasions when the designer guards the edge of the green on all sides because the golfer has a short approach or tee shot. The surrounding bunkers make the shot a hit-or-miss affair. Miss the green, and you're in a bunker or worse. This unique pattern is less commonly used than the other patterns mentioned, but two good examples illustrating this defense are the 103-yard seventh at Pebble Beach and the 131-yard tenth at our Chateau Whistler course.

What You Should Know About Sand's Physical Characteristics

It's safe to assume that you'll experience your share of bunker shots. Sand appears on courses because either nature or the designer has put it there. Generally speaking, designers work with available materials, so the sand you find on the course is likely to be a local variety. It is the exception to import "foreign" sand, although it is done.

Bunker sand selection is guided by a number of considerations, including wind (in windy areas we use a heavier type so that it doesn't blow out), weather (in areas with frequent rain, we use a porous type that drains and dries more quickly), and slope (on slopes we use a sand with drainage and compaction characteristics that minimize sliding). Finally, designers consider color content and aesthetics.

Probably the easiest way to understand how we select sand is to study three projects with different requirements. On rare occasions at our Four Seasons Resort Nevis the wind can gust fiercely and it can rain buckets in a couple of hours. The sand on such a course needs to drain well and not blow away when the wind whips up, so we chose a heavy, coarse sand. At the Golf Club de Grenoble, in Grenoble, France, our choice was a softer, finer sand to give golfers the chance to play higher, softer shots to the many elevated, undulating greens. Third, at Spanish Trail Golf and Country Club in Las Vegas, we used a combination of the Nevis and Grenoble sand types, with the texture resembling the surrounding desert.

As a general playing rule, the best way to determine the type of sand you are confronting is to use your feet. As you enter the bunker, concentrate on feeling the texture and the depth of the sand. Does it give way easily, making deep footprints, or does it support your shoe? You are allowed to set your feet firmly in the sand to get secure footing. Working your feet into the sand can tell you a lot about its resistance qualities and what kind of shot you need to hit for a good recovery.

The four most common types of bunker sand are coral, limestone, river, and silica. Identifying the sand is one factor that will help you decide how hard you need to swing.

Coral sand is found in the tropics and on islands. The loose, large particles are almost shell-like in some cases. It seldom produces a buried lie.

Limestone, an inland cousin to coral, can be ground into sand of various grades, from a very fine or powdery type to a larger, coarser type. Generally, the softer and deeper the sand is spread the greater chance for a buried lie; odds are, though, you will have a

AT FOUR SEASONS RESORT NEVIS IN THE CARIBBEAN, A HEAVY, COARSE SAND IS UTILIZED IN THE BUNKERS.

126

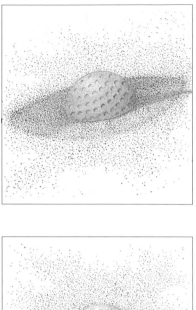

When confronted with a "fried egg" lie, expect the ball to run once it lands.

Clean lies in the sand allow you to control the ball better, assuming the proper recovery technique is applied.

good lie. Limestone sand usually allows you to generate substantial backspin.

River sands are the product of many parent materials. These sands are often round and hard. Such sands are commonly used in bunkers as they are local, durable, and drain well. The playing characteristics will vary depending on source, size, particle distribution, and other factors. The ball tends to sit up reasonably well on this sand type.

High-purity silica sand is often very white, lending sharp contrast to the scene on the course. The particles tend to be rounded, increasing your chances of a "fried egg" lie — that is, a ball buried halfway in the sand. Explosion shots out of silica sand rarely spin well.

You should also keep in mind that the playing characteristics of dry sand and wet sand are distinctly different. Dry sand tends to be less firm and can cause you to bury your club behind the ball. Use an aggressive swing, take a minimal amount of sand, and make sure to follow through. Conversely, wet sand is more compacted, and the club will often bounce off its surface, causing you to skull or blade shots. Swing softer and take less sand because the ball will come out low and fast.

For most players, bunkers are scary and intimidating — unless you love the beach. But they are an architect's best gambit for providing definition and creating strategy on a golf course. Often, a bunker will save you additional strokes, provided you know how to escape. Last, in many instances sand can be "friendly" if you understand how the designer is using it. Water and trees, on the other hand, are rarely friendly, as you will find out in the next chapter.

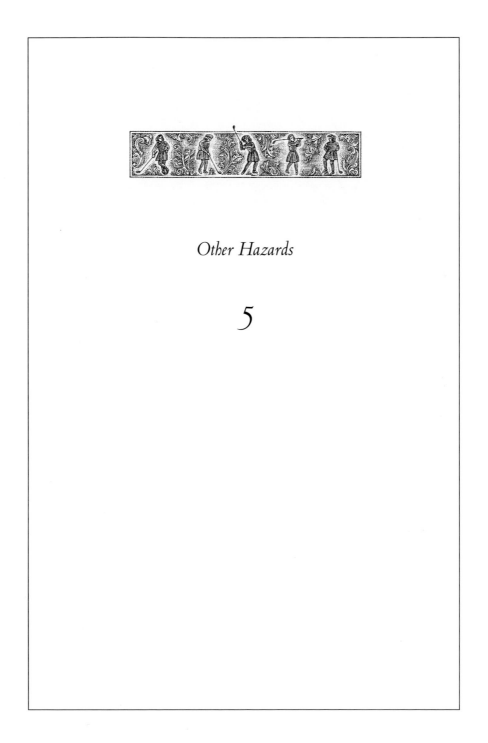

Other Hazards

5

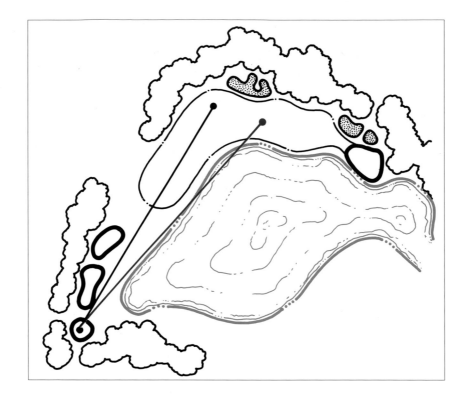

The par-4 third hole at Shanghai Country
Club in China contains a major water hazard
that forces golfers to assess their options.

PRECEDING PAGE:

A LARGE WATER HAZARD FLANKS

THE LEFT SIDE OF THE PAR-5 TWELFTH

HOLE AT CHENAL COUNTRY CLUB.

 In 1981, I was approached by the owners of an unusual property near the city of Perth, Australia. They wanted to know if it would be suitable for a golf course of international standard. As we walked the land together for the first time, it was obvious to me that a truly exceptional and spectacular course could be created, and the Joondalup Country Club began to take shape in my mind. The site combined three different settings: one portion was fairly gentle with tall stands of indigenous eucalyptus trees and native grasses; another embraced rolling sand dunes interspersed with natural dune vegetation; and the rest consisted of rugged, rocky terrain out of which several stone quarries had been carved.

One of these abandoned quarries was considerably wider and deeper than the others, and the owners had begun filling in parts of it. It immediately struck me that this forbidding chasm, properly incorporated into the golf course, would be a splendid hazard that players would not easily disregard or forget. I described my concept to the owners, who promptly ceased their filling efforts. Today this awe-inspiring feature is an integral part of Joondalup's 149-yard par-3 third hole.

Why did the quarry's hazard potential excite me so much? The answer to this question involves a lesson in how designers use hazards. Once you understand this lesson, your ability to handle them will improve.

"Hazard"— the very word conjures up notions of peril, fear, and jeopardy. These are, indeed, the emotions golf hazards are intended to evoke. In turn, these emotions decrease the probability that you will decisively select and execute the appropriate shot. By learning how designers use hazards, you will be able, in many circumstances, to reduce or eliminate the negative thoughts frequently associated with them.

The beauty of a hazard, if you can learn to think of it this way, is that you are not necessarily in for trouble. It's merely the possibility of trouble that you are worried about. A famous line from the legendary golfer Bobby Jones sums it up: "The value of any hazard is oftentimes more psychological than penal."

The only areas classified as hazards by the Rules of Golf are bunkers and water hazards. But for this discussion, I'll consider a hazard to be any area that you are consciously trying to avoid because of your perception that escape from it will be difficult or impossible. In other words, it is a forbidding area as far as you and your game are concerned. Therefore, the concept is often quite personal in the sense that an area constituting a severe hazard for one player may not be a hazard for another due to disparities in their shot-making skills. Sidehill lies, for example, may be a troublesome hazard for some golfers, but of little or no consequence for skilled players. And, as you saw in the last chapter, for expert sand players a friendly bunker is about as fearsome as the briar patch was for Brer Rabbit.

On the other hand, some hazards are absolute in the sense that escape is impossible except in the rarest of situations, and once you are in them your only course of action is to drop a ball and take a penalty. Out-of-bounds, lakes, chasms, jungles, oceans, and rivers typify inescapable hazards. But you should also be alert to the existence of another type of hazard, often much less dramatic in appearance, that may be even more damaging to your score than an inescapable hazard. For example, exceptionally deep rough or severely penal bunkers may cost you far more strokes than a lake or a pond. These less striking hazards will also have you pulling out your hair at a much faster rate from frustration due to their initially innocent appearance. However, when you are on Joondalup's third tee, staring down into the 80-foot-deep quarry, the situation may well evoke all the golfer's feelings of peril and jeopardy. Clearly, a ball struck into this gorge is lost. The hazard has produced

AT THE PAR-3 THIRD HOLE ON JOONDALUP'S QUARRY NINE, THE DEPTH OF THE LARGE QUARRY CAN BE VISUALLY INTIMIDATING, BUT THE ACTUAL CARRY ACROSS THIS HAZARD IS RELATIVELY BENIGN.

precisely the effect I intended: if you teed off now, your anxiety would likely result in a poor club choice or a misstruck ball.

Now, however, with me as your guide, you are going to examine this particular hazard in more detail before teeing off. Although it is unsettling to contemplate falling into the quarry (which probably, at least subconsciously, is running through your mind), your initial thoughts should focus on your attack options rather than the question of whether a parachute would open before you hit bottom. This hazard falls into the category of hazards that cannot be circumvented — you must play over the quarry or end up in it.

With no alternative available, the abyss must be carried. You must now determine the required shot's degree of difficulty. From the preceding photo, you can see that the shot is actually relatively simple. This situation is the norm rather than the exception; that is, when a hazard must be carried, the required shot often is not difficult if, but only if, you do not let the hazard completely capture your attention. Designer Alister Mackenzie described the essence of many hazards when he observed, "It is an important thing in golf to make holes look much more difficult than they really are. People receive great pleasure in challenging a hole which looks virtually impossible and yet is not so difficult as it appears."

The trick, then, is to recognize the required shot's level of difficulty and be able to minimize or disregard the hazard's existence. When there is no option available, you should anticipate that the required shot probably will be easier than it appears at first glance.

Almost all hazards, whether natural or created, will afford you options. Unlike the quarry on Joondalup's third hole, where there is no option, the vast majority of hazards present a number of shot-making choices. To determine your proper method of attack, you need to understand the physical characteristics of each hazard and how they relate to your individual shot-making skills. By

IF YOU ARE NOT CAREFUL, THE VEGETATION AND SCENERY CAN DISTRACT YOU AT THE PAR-3 SEVENTH HOLE ON PRINCEVILLE'S PRINCE COURSE.

"Inescapable" hazards like the large lake on the par-5 twelfth hole at Kinojo Country Club in Japan offer no chance for recovery.

comprehending the effects of angle, location, and size, you will be better equipped to select your optimum route.

First, identify the precise perimeter of any hazard. This is extremely important if its shape is irregular. Then, note the characteristics of the terrain adjacent to the hazard and determine how they will influence a shot landing there. For example, a pond may serve to collect runoff, so all the adjacent terrain slopes into it.

Next, you should assess the severity of escape. Is it an inescapable hazard like a lake or an out-of-bounds? Remember, designers can make difficult hazards look easy and, alternatively, can make relatively easy hazards appear very difficult. A small pot bunker may look harmless but, in fact, may be deeper than it seems and harbor steep sides that preclude any shot except a short escape shot. Conversely, a large, flat, maintained sandy waste area that is larger than the fairway may seem intimidating, but escape is relatively easy.

Taking into consideration the hazard's escape severity and its location, identify a target area that will both (1) "give you a good leave," in pool terms — that is, afford you a good subsequent shot, and (2) provide a comfortable landing zone where you can confidently put the ball. The two skills that are absolutely critical for proficient hazard management are the ability to calculate accurate distances on the golf course and knowing how far you can reasonably expect to hit each club.

The par-3 sixteenth hole at Cypress Point Club will certainly intensify any golfer's heartbeat.

I have already discussed several mechanical ways to sharpen your ability to calculate distances, including the use of yardage books, making your own yardage guide, and benefiting from the laser-measured distances marked on sprinkler heads. In the event that a yardage book or a sprinkler head is not available, try breaking the total distance into segments and then add them together to produce a reasonable estimate. For example, if there is a lake between you and the hole, figure out how far you are from the water's edge. Then, calculate the distance across the hazard to the front portion of the green. The total should provide you with a reasonable estimate.

You can also improve your ability to eyeball distances more accurately through a number of drills. For example, before you check your yardage book or a sprinkler head, get into the habit of estimating the distance you are about to check and then see how accurate you were. Also get accustomed to using your time on the practice range to fine-tune your distance-calculating skills. (Later, I will discuss situations involving illusions and other circumstances that may impede your ability to correctly calculate distances.)

Your knowledge of the average distance you hit each club is just as important as your skill in calculating yardage. Obviously, it does you no good to determine that you need a 165-yard shot to carry a hazard if you select a club that you can hit only 150 yards. The practice range is the ideal place for you to master this unique aspect of your own game. Every serious player should take the time and effort necessary to develop a personal club-distance chart. It will let you know how far you can expect to hit each club — an invaluable tool in many situations.

The intellectual Dr. Mackenzie, writing on the subject of hazards, said, "Most golfers have an erroneous view of the real object of hazards. The majority of them simply look upon a hazard as a means of punishing a bad shot, whereas their real object is to make the game more interesting. For example, players get such a tremendous thrill driving over the ocean at the spectacular 222-yard par-3

ON THE PAR-4 NINTH HOLE AT WISLEY'S GARDEN
NINE, YOU SHOULD AVOID THE WATER ON THE LEFT EVEN AT
THE EXPENSE OF LANDING IN THE RIGHT-SIDE BUNKERS.

sixteenth hole at Cypress Point that this also is well worth the risk of losing a ball or two. I recently traveled from England with an American who told me that the sixteenth at Cypress Point had cost him a fortune in golf balls because he would always play for the long carry to the green across the ocean. However, the joy of seeing his ball land on the green and the feeling of achievement in successfully negotiating this major hazard was worth all the balls he put into the ocean in his attempts to carry the hazard."

Hazards are like spices that a designer sprinkles on a course to give it flavor. Without them, golf courses would be terribly boring. Even though players complain about hazards, they return to those courses and holes that fairly challenge them, and, more often than not, a great hazard is the magnet that brings them back.

On the Wisley Golf Club's Garden Nine just outside London, England, we created a number of hazards to add character and flavor to a parcel of land that was basically flat with few trees. For example, we took the 364-yard par-4 ninth hole, which could have been a plain, routine dogleg, and added a large lake on the inside and clusters of bunkers on the outside. Presto — there is now plenty of drama for any golfer.

WATER

Water on a golf course normally comes in the form of (1) rivers, streams, and creeks, (2) lakes and ponds, (3) oceans, and (4) marshes and wetlands. In making your shot selection in the face of a water hazard, you should take into account its location, its angle with respect to the hole's centerline, and its shape. Disregard any of these characteristics and you may well end up drenched.

With respect to the hole's centerline, the hazard will be perpendicular, parallel, diagonal, or bending (where the hole's configuration is around a water body located on the inside of the angle). A water hazard's location may be near the tee, in or adjacent to the fairway, or near the green. It can have virtually any shape imaginable.

The 367-yard par-4 fourteenth hole at Sugarloaf in Carrabassett, Maine, demonstrates the use of water in a perpendicular manner. A stream crosses the fairway at a virtual right angle in relation to the configuration of the fairway and green. Water used in this fashion forces players to carry the ball a certain distance to negotiate the trouble, depending on their position and where the hazard is located. In this particular case, players must carry the approach shot to the green or suffer the consequences.

On the 413-yard par-4 fourth hole at Glencoe Golf and Country Club in Calgary, Alberta, a rocky creek hugs the entire left side of the hole, and players who successfully challenge it can take a bunker guarding the front right side of the green out of play. The key is knowing where the inside edge of the creek is located and being able to put your ball near it. If you challenge this hazard and are successful, an improved angle of approach is the reward. But for many golfers, the prudent play is safely down the right side of the fairway, taking little chance that water will claim the ball.

FOLLOWING PAGE:
THE LEFT SIDE OF THE PAR-4 FOURTH HOLE AT GLENCOE'S GLEN FOREST COURSE IN CANADA IS DEFENDED BY A PARALLEL WATER HAZARD.

Now take a look at the 422-yard par-4 third hole at our Deer Creek course in Overland Park, Kansas, which typifies a designer's use of a diagonal water hazard. As the diagram shows, the creek diagonally bisects the fairway. The line of your shot should be carefully planned because shots of equal length will clear or encounter the hazard depending on their lines.

The 576-yard par-5 thirteenth hole at The Dunes, illustrated in Chapter 2 and designed by my father, is a good example of a bending challenge. Standing on the tee, with a vast expanse of water stretching along the right side of the fairway and at a 90-degree (horseshoe) angle around to the green, you will first note that an alternative route down the left side of the hole will allow you to play around the water at the expense of lengthening the hole considerably. On the other hand, if you challenge the water, you must decide how much of the hazard to cut off.

In addition, remember that, frequently, water hazards are not configured as neat, simple, geometric figures but as irregular, haphazard forms. They may have inlets, fingers, and other jagged features requiring a carry of an additional several yards or more than would be the case if the hazard's edge were smoothly shaped. You should carefully discern if the hazard in question possesses irregular shape features that call for a longer carry than appears to be needed at first glance. If so, then factor this consideration into your shot selection. Judging distance over water can be very misleading because the flattening effect of a large body of water makes the distance over it appear different than it actually is. Be extra thorough in your distance calculation and ensure that you use a club that will get you over the water.

Also, you should always check to see if the land adjacent to the water hazard is contoured so that balls landing there will be guided toward or into the hazard. This situation is not uncommon because, for example, a water hazard often is a component of the course's drainage system and is situated in a low area. Thus, if the land flows

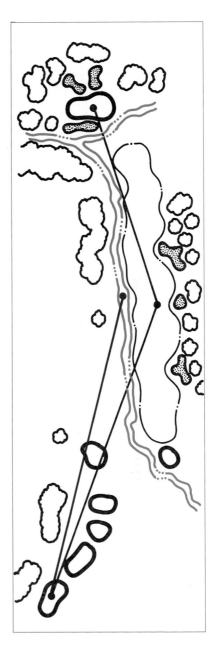

Diagonal water hazards, such as the creek on the par-4 third hole at Deer Creek Golf Course, tempt golfers to "bite off what they can chew" without getting wet.

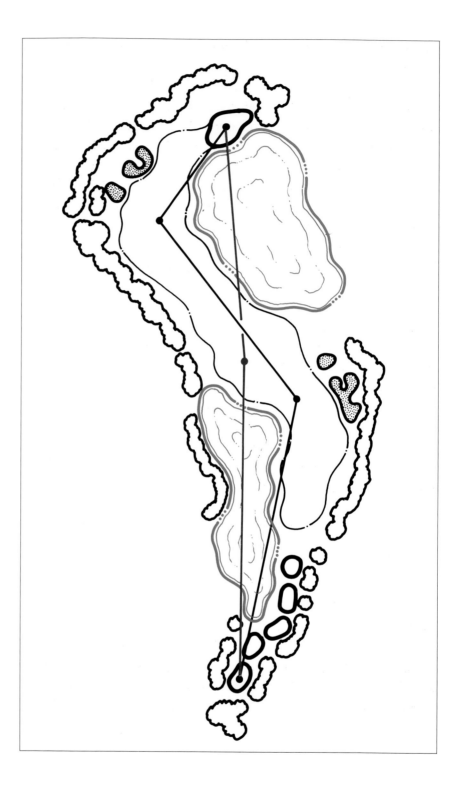

At Brookside Country Club's par-5 sixteenth hole, two lakes were created to introduce risk and reward, but the amount of gamble is up to you.

toward the hazard, be sure to consider this factor when making your shot selection.

Occasionally, water is encountered on a hole in two or three locations. As the accompanying sketch reveals, we used this design technique for the 559-yard par-5 sixteenth hole at our Brookside course. We constructed two man-made lakes, one off the tee and another near the green, to dramatize the tee, second, and third shots. This situation tempts golfers into playing near or over water at least two and possibly three times. You have the option of taking a heroic route close to or over the water's edge, thus shortening the hole and significantly improving the angle of play. Obviously, this route does not come without risk.

Whenever golfers are required to play a penal shot directly over a severe hazard, the designer normally gives careful attention to ensuring that the obstacle is challenging yet fair. As I mentioned earlier, although some water hazards may be visually intimidating at first glance, the effect designers relish is that the required shot may be surprisingly easy. However, this is not necessarily the case with a heroic shot such as the one facing you on Brookside's sixteenth hole. Here, I have created a significant carry across the second lake that protects the green, but also have given you the option to circumvent the water by using the portion of fairway that wraps around the lake's left side. If you are in doubt as to your ability to successfully negotiate the heroic route, you should take the safe route.

On par-3 holes designers occasionally position water in a penal fashion. The notion is that it is acceptable to challenge you to make a difficult shot if you are afforded the perfect lie that the tee provides, as I discussed in Chapter 2. At the Medinah Country Club in the 1990 U.S. Open, we saw a situation in which competitors were faced three times (Nos. 2, 13, and 17) with substantial carries over water.

Three of the four par-3's on Medinah Country Club's No. 3 Course feature water that must be carried.

#2

#13

#17

When faced with a carry over water, you must constantly be aware of your lie. For example, trying to hit from a downslope across a water hazard is a low-percentage shot for most golfers. A bad lie says be conservative. If you're striking the ball well and have a decent lie, be aggressive. But don't try to execute shots you are almost incapable of hitting. Laying up is not to be confused with chickening out. The first law of lay-ups is if you're going to lay up, lay up. In other words, make sure you wind up short of the hazard with a good angle for your next shot.

Equally important to the golfer's decision-making process is the location of water on different areas of the hole. For example, designers generally incorporate water near a tee to distract golfers, but seldom to penalize them unless a major mistake is made.

Generally, water near a fairway is intended to tempt you to play close to it in order to obtain a preferred angle of attack or an advantage in distance on your next stroke. This decision relates back to your determination of the various risks and rewards in a given situation. Although less significant than the risk-reward equation, another reason water is located adjacent to a landing area can simply be to capture poorly planned or executed shots. Finally, when water is placed directly across the fairway, the designer is asking if you can play safely across or should you take a conservative approach and play short.

Water fronting a green is commonly utilized and poses one of golf's toughest shots. Not only are you trying to clear water, but you must also land and stop the ball safely on the green. A basic rule of thumb is to make sure you select a club that will carry the hazard. This decision can mean different choices depending upon skill levels. Highly skilled players often hit full shots in this situation and will choose a club they must hit solid. Most golfers, however, should pick a club that gives them margin for error.

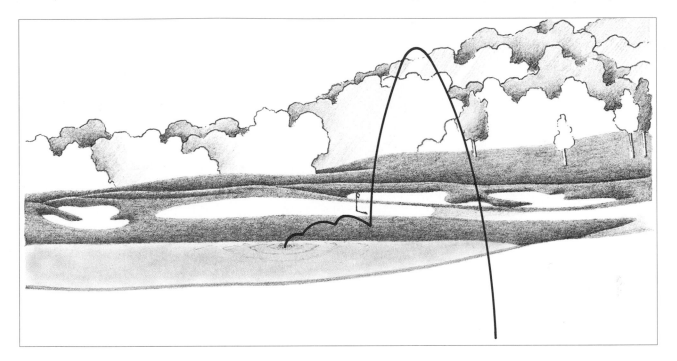

The 625-yard par-5 sixteenth hole at Firestone Country Club illustrates this type of situation. The lake is nestled up close to the edge of the putting surface with only a thin strip of rough separating the water from the green. Any mishit or slight miscalculation by the golfer will put the ball in a watery grave. Take extra care and analyze all available information (yardage, wind, moisture, and temperature) before selecting a club. When making your final determination, remember that even the best players in the world often factor in a cushion and reach for an extra club. If they are willing to hit the ball to the back of the green in this situation, you should be, too.

A good way to block out water fronting a green is to focus on a noticeable feature behind it, such as the edge of a bunker, a tree, or a mound, and play to a distance on the rear of the green. Designers often incorporate features behind a green for visual definition, and smart golfers make good use of them. By shifting your attention to this area, the water hazard in front will become secondary to your

Certain buffer zones, like the area on the par-5 thirteenth hole at Sun Rise Country Club in Yang Mei, Taiwan, offer no chance for recovery.

thought process, and its potential for generating negative pre-shot thoughts will be diminished. Expert players have been using this method for years.

Water surrounding a green is a rarity and offers little or no room for error. The two most common situations in which designers utilize this configuration are (1) on a relatively short par-3 and (2) on a par-5 that calls for a short approach shot. The basic rule is to calculate the distance to the middle of the green and aim for it. Shooting for a flagstick located close to the water's edge is exactly what the designer is tempting you to do. On rare occasions, a bailout area might be available, but don't count on it. The penal quality of this type of hole is unparalleled and calls for conservative shot selection.

When hitting to a green, always pay special attention to what we designers refer to as the "buffer zone" — the area between the perimeter of the water hazard and the edge of the putting surface. This zone may be a slope, a bunker, a mound, or simply a flat area. Oftentimes, golfers anticipate that carrying the water hazard will guarantee good results, but they fail to factor in the additional distance between the edge of the water and the front of the putting surface. Ending up in this area can provide some unpleasant surprises, such as the necessity of escaping from deep rough.

The 520-yard par-5 eleventh hole at Spyglass Hill Golf Course illustrates this point. A major buffer zone about 20 yards wide is situated between the putting surface and the large pond guarding the front of the green. The buffer zone, in turn, consists of a fairly steep slope with a healthy cut of rough on it. Always be on the alert for these buffer zones and factor them into your shot and club selection.

It is important to understand the total nature of a buffer zone. Thick grass along a body of water, for example, may save a misplayed shot from going into the water and let you recover. On the other hand, rocks, penal rough, or other unforgiving material won't give you any help. When selecting a club in these situations, allow a little room for error to ensure carrying the hazard and the buffer zone.

One of the most incredible narrow escapes from a water hazard occurred at the 1975 Canadian Open. Playing off the tee at the 426-yard par-4 sixteenth hole at Royal Montreal Golf Club in Quebec, pro Pat Fitzsimons struck a wild tee shot that landed on a tiny island in the middle of a large pond. Because the lake was reasonably shallow, his caddie was able to wade across the water with Fitzsimons on his shoulders. Upon arrival, Fitzsimons played his second shot to the green and miraculously saved par. It was one pair of pants Fitzsimons didn't mind ruining, especially considering his trademark was old corduroys.

No matter how diligently you have prepared yourself to combat the perils of water hazards, remember that no one is immune from disaster. In the 1985 Masters, Curtis Strange was breezing along and seemed a sure winner until his second shots at the par-5 thirteenth and fifteenth holes wound up wet. In the 1986 Masters, Seve Ballesteros saw his hopes for a third green jacket drown when he found the water with his second shot at No. 15, opening the door for Jack Nicklaus's sixth title. Normally, golfers don't recover from water. There are, however, exceptions. In the 1983 Masters, Ballesteros successfully extricated a partially submerged ball from Rae's Creek on the 465-yard par-5 thirteenth hole. After taking off one shoe and putting on his rain pants to protect himself from the large splash, he played a magnificent blast, which, at the time, kept his momentum intact and later, as he explained, was the shot that propelled him to victory.

On many great courses, the most dramatic, eye-catching features are trees. Although golfers generally think of them as hazards, you should keep in mind that they serve many other purposes, including functioning as visual or sound screens, lending aesthetic value, preserving habitat, and acting as safety barriers against errant shots. In addition, designers occasionally use trees to assist you with your shot selection or execution. For example, trees can indicate the proper shot line or serve as the backdrop for a green to help you calculate distances. In summary, don't anticipate that your game plan will have to factor in every tree as a hazard.

The first thing you should ask yourself when facing a tree or a group of trees is whether a slightly mishit or misaligned shot may strike them or end up under or behind one of them in a position that will substantially impede the next shot. If you answer this question yes, then this tree or group of trees squarely fits the definition of a hazard, because you are now facing an area of the golf course that you want to avoid.

Whereas water presents you with a two-dimensional hazard, trees confront you with a three-dimensional challenge. Because of the third dimension, these vertical hazards often require a much more complex shot-selection process: if you plan to play over, under, or through a tree or stand of trees, you not only must select the proper line and calculate the distance but you must also determine the required shot altitude. On the other hand, if you are going to "shape" your shot around a tree hazard, such as a large tree on the inside of a dogleg, then you must calculate the right-to-left or left-to-right curvature that is required. Then you must execute this three-parameter shot, which, obviously, can be much more difficult than a two-parameter (line and distance) shot.

When you are at the practice range, you should devote some effort to finding out how high you can expect to hit each club, as well as

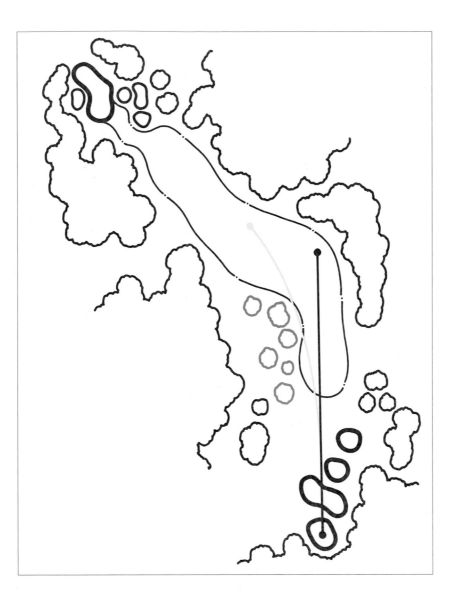

*Trees are often used in the formation of
doglegs, and golfers who can curve the ball
appropriately will gain a significant advantage.*

what kind of shape you can produce. Consider taking a lesson from your local PGA professional to understand the fundamentals of trajectory and shape. This knowledge will help you successfully tackle the three dimensional challenge posed by tree hazards.

Recognizing that shots involving tree hazards can be tricky, you should carefully assess the degree of difficulty, in relation to your shot-making skills, of going over, under, around, or through the tree hazard in question. If the difficulty factor is high, you should analyze the situation to see if you can avoid making a frontal attack. In other words, just as in chess, think a few moves ahead to see if the proper current move is partially dictated by the following move's alternatives. By correctly factoring in the next shot's potential tree problems, you may be able to avoid them completely by your choice of shot line or laying up.

On heavily wooded sites, a tree-clearing operation creates fairway corridors. Here, designers oftentimes bend the fairway by the way they clear the trees. This technique frequently creates a shot-making decision for the player, because a bending or curved hole may require the player to either lay up off the tee or shape a longer shot to fit the hole.

Consider a hole that bends to the left in the shape of a banana with the wooded area on the outside edge being, say, only 210 yards from the tee. Also assume that the hole is a 430-yard par-4. You must now decide to hit the tee shot 200 yards straightaway, leaving a 230-yard shot to the green, or play a right-to-left shot around the inside tree line and short of the outside tree line, thereby leaving a shorter shot to the green. If you can shape your shot to the movement of the hole, you can gain a substantial advantage.

Sites that contain sporadic or intermittent stands of trees pose a great challenge to the designer in determining how best to incorporate them. For many golfers, single trees and small clusters often present difficult decisions for determining whether challenging

The lone oak at the par-4
twelfth at Stanford University Golf
Course in California has a major
influence on the strategy of the hole.

them is worthwhile. Small stands or groves of trees can be used to guard almost any portion of a golf hole, from tee through green. For example, a single grove of trees might be positioned near the driving area to require a shot over, under, around, or away. Or a stand of trees may be placed next to a green site to guard a corner of the putting surface. Either way, their presence means you must ask yourself whether you gain a significant advantage by successfully challenging them and how difficult is escape should you find yourself in them.

Occasionally, a single tree is an important component of a hole's strategy. This result is achieved in a number of ways. A designer can place a lone tree in the first landing area to make a tee shot tighter, thus requiring increased accuracy. Such a tree also requires the player to decide to play left or right. The 364-yard par-4 second hole at Coto de Caza in California's Orange County features an oak tree that serves to narrow the driving area significantly: golfers can gamble by favoring the right side of this oak and a nearby collection bunker, or play to the left, which is a much safer route. If they gamble and are successful, they are rewarded with a shorter approach shot and a better angle to the green. If they play safe off the tee, they are left with a much tougher approach shot over trees and a bunker.

You may also find a tree located beyond the first landing area on the edge of a fairway that appears innocuous from the tee. When you analyze, as in pool, what kind of "leave" you will have for your second shot, this tree may suddenly take on great importance. A good example can be found on the 358-yard par-4 thirteenth hole at Harbour Town Golf Links on Hilton Head Island, South Carolina, site of the PGA Tour's Heritage Classic. A large tree on the left edge of the fairway limits the advantageous driving area to the right half of the fairway, because balls struck to the left half will require you to play around, over, or under this tree.

Sometimes you will encounter a lone tree located directly in the center of the fairway either at or beyond the first landing area. Deciding how to deal with such a tree can be very confusing, but usually the other features on the hole offer some clues as to the optimum route. The 470-yard par-4 twelfth hole at the Stanford University Golf Club in California has a large oak centered at 340 yards off the tee. In this case, due to the hole's length, many golfers will play directly at the tree and worry about avoiding it on their next shot.

Finally, a single tree may guard a corner of a green surface and make a portion of that green inaccessible from certain locations in the fairway. A large pecan tree known as Big Annie stood on the 387-yard par-4 seventeenth hole at the Colonial Country Club in Fort Worth, Texas, obstructing the approach to the green from the right-hand side of the fairway. The tree was lost in a severe storm, and the playability of the hole changed dramatically. Accordingly, although a single tree may make for some interesting shot-making choices, designers must make difficult decisions when considering a single tree as the primary feature for a hole because a storm or disease may someday eliminate it.

Trees, unlike other features, constantly change height, width, and shape due to natural growth, diseases, insects, aging, storms, pruning, and other causes. Thus, it is likely that a tree or stand of trees will perform a specific strategic role on a hole for only a limited period of time, and then changes in the trees, whether gradual or sudden, will alter the hole's playing characteristics.

The Colonial Country Club — close to the home of the legendary Ben Hogan, long considered to be the master of controlling the shape and trajectory of golf shots — is a course dominated by rows of dense trees on every fairway, and a player who is able to control shape and trajectory has a great advantage. It is widely believed that Hogan honed his incredible shot-making skills by playing the course frequently during his competitive days. Like Hogan, you should utilize every opportunity to improve your play on heavily treed courses by analyzing thoroughly each shot that may encounter a tree or group of trees.

Water and tree hazards pose a variety of playing challenges. Both of them, if improperly handled, will inflate your score and give you fits in the process. But if you understand their function and purpose, they can serve as guides to better shot making.

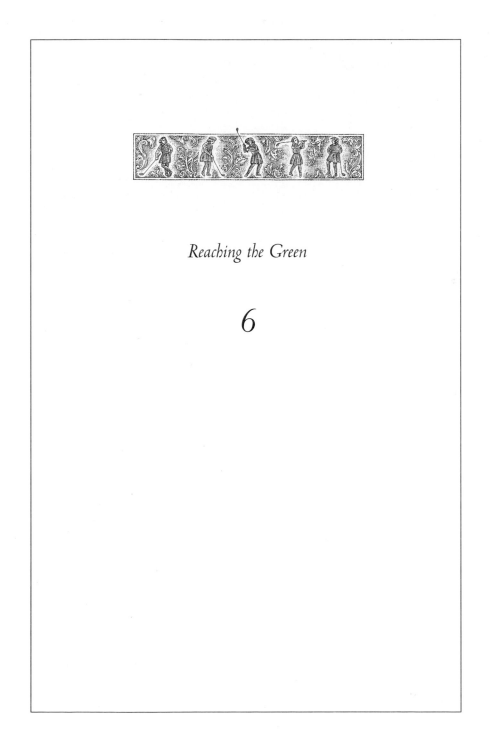

Reaching the Green

6

SHORT PAR-3S OFTEN HAVE SEVERE HAZARDS, LIKE
REVETTED BUNKERS, MOUNDING, AND DEEP
SWALES AT TROON'S EIGHTH HOLE IN SCOTLAND.

PRECEDING PAGE:
THE PAR-4 FOURTH HOLE AT WAILEA'S
ORANGE COURSE IS WELL DEFENDED BY A SERIES
OF BUNKERS NEAR THE GREEN COMPLEX.

Now let's see how you use your increased understanding of hazards and other features to improve decision making and execution connected with the "approach shot," that is, the shot the designer intends you to hit to the green. We will focus on the landing area (the area from which the designer expects you to approach the green) and the green complex (the green and areas adjacent to it). In determining the hazards a designer will incorporate into the landing area and the green complex, the key consideration is the length of the expected approach shot. As length decreases, you can typically expect to encounter more hazards of increasing severity.

With par-4 and par-5 holes you should be alert for hazards in both the landing area and the green complex. With par-3s there generally is no landing area because you execute your shot to the green from a tee. Thus, with par-3s you can create a perfect lie, develop a preferred stance, and adjust the attack angle to suit your game by choosing where to place your ball between the tee markers. If the shot is short, the designer may feel it is fair to incorporate severely penal hazards into the green complex. Take the 126-yard par-3 eighth hole at Troon on Scotland's Ayrshire coast. Nicknamed the Postage Stamp, it features a small green surrounded by deep bunkers, hummocks, and swales from which escape is extremely difficult. It is rare to encounter such a penal test in a par-4 or par-5 green complex because your approach-shot lie, stance, and angle will almost always be less than ideal.

What can you anticipate on par-4s and par-5s regarding the landing area? If the approach shot is relatively short, the designer may place significant hazards in the landing area to punish a poor shot. For example, the fairway may be narrowed by rough or bunkers to force golfers to consider playing either well short to a safer area or long enough to carry beyond the trouble.

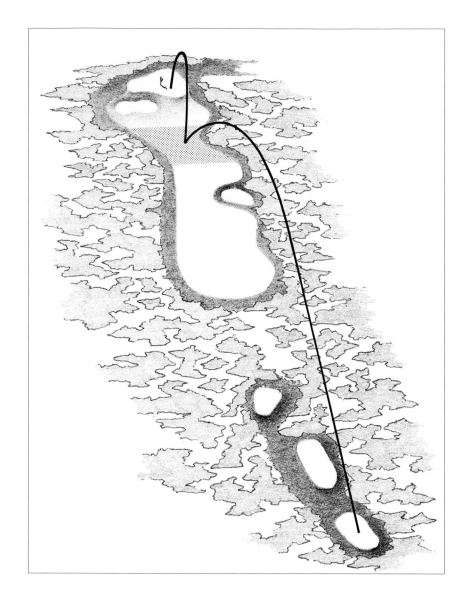

*On Spanish Bay's short par-4
second, trouble abounds in the landing
area and also near the green.*

The drawing of the 307-yard par-4 second hole at Spanish Bay shows how we used this narrowing technique where sand dunes, native plants, and a lone fairway bunker squeeze the landing area for the final 100 yards. The green is also guarded by sand dunes in the rear and on the sides as well as by a large deep bunker in the front left. This type of scenario, with challenging hazards in both the landing area and the green complex, is more the rule than the exception with short par-4s.

On the other hand, the 450-yard par-4 fifth hole at Jefferson Golf and Country Club in Columbus, Ohio, illustrates the type of situation you will often encounter with a long approach shot. For the approach shot on this lengthy par-4, most players must use either a fairway wood or a long iron — clubs that are more difficult to control. As the drawing shows, even though the landing area is bunkered on both sides, the fairway is wide.

APPROACHING THE SIXTEENTH GREEN AT HYATT COOLUM RESORT IN AUSTRALIA REQUIRES PINPOINT ACCURACY DUE TO BUNKERING, GRASSY HOLLOWS, AND A SMALL, SLOPING GREEN.

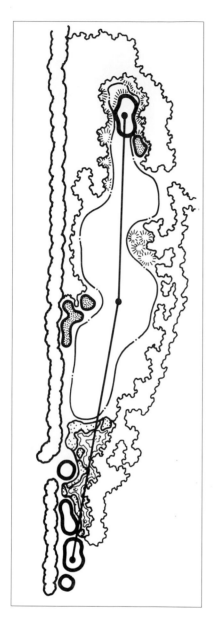

The par-4 fifth hole at Jefferson Golf and Country Club in Columbus, Ohio, incorporates softer defenses, allowing golfers a chance for recovery.

To compensate for the demanding approach shot, I placed some "friendly" mounds and swales around the green that are easy to play from, making recovery play relatively simple. The fairway also connects directly with the green so that players can bounce or roll the ball onto the putting surface. You can see that, in light of the approach shot's substantial length, the green complex presents a gentle and receptive setting.

Now take a look at the landing area and green complex of the short 350-yard par-4 sixteenth hole at the Hyatt Coolum Resort in Coolum, Australia. Many golfers, including those playing from forward tees, will approach this green from a distance of 100 yards or less. Thus, a strong defense is required. Two bunkers have been placed in the landing area about 90 yards from the green to challenge players of all skill levels. If you find one, it takes near perfect execution to reach the green in a single stroke, even for expert players. In addition, two more bunkers and some deep grassy hollows tightly guard the steeply elevated green. Each of these hazards poses a problem if entered, and you should develop a playing strategy to minimize your chances of ending up in them. The small plateaued green also requires substantial precision.

Bunkers positioned 40 or more yards from the green present one of golf's most difficult playing challenges. Generally, the safest escape from a bunker is an "explosion" shot using a sand wedge that blasts the ball out of the bunker by lifting the sand under it without any actual ball-club contact. Unfortunately, 40 yards is beyond the range of an explosion shot. To have any chance of reaching the green in one shot, you will have to make precise ball-club contact, which brings into play factors that are difficult to predict. Depending on distance and your lie, reaching the green in one stroke can present a formidable challenge.

As you walk toward the green complex, you may have an opportunity to get a detailed look at important playing characteristics of

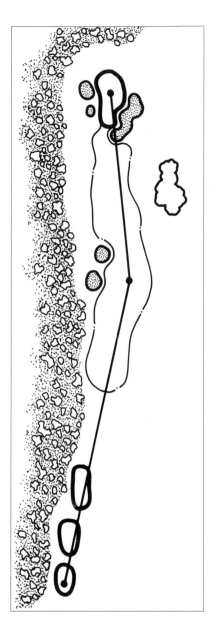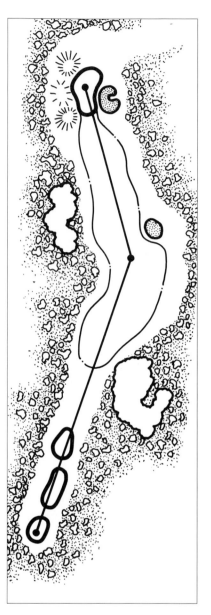

*Although similar in length,
the second and fourth holes at the
Desert Dunes Golf Course
have different defenses in their design.*

features that were not apparent from farther away. For example, rough may be taller, bunkers may be deeper or steeper, and slopes may be more inclined than you'd imagined. You also can discover features you hadn't even noticed before, like grassy hollows, pot bunkers, or subtle mounds. By observing these characteristics in closer detail, you'll be able to form a clearer picture of their potential effects on your approach shot.

Designers don't enjoy repetitious or monotonous settings any more than you do. Therefore, it is unlikely that two par-4s of the same length on a course will be defended in the same way. So be alert for rhythm changes intended to give each hole its own personality.

The second and the fourth holes at Desert Dunes Golf Course illustrate the use of different hazard concepts on similar holes. Both are just over 400 yards long, and the approach shots play about the same length. The approach shot on the second hole is strongly defended by bunkers at the green, while the fourth hole has only a single bunker protecting its putting surface. I positioned these hazards based on three considerations: (1) the tee shot on the second hole is less demanding due to the forgiving landing area on the right; (2) the bunkers in the green complex on the second hole require golfers to execute an aerial approach shot; and (3) on the fourth hole, stronger contouring of the putting surface makes it much more challenging, so I softened the defenses in the green complex to counterbalance it.

When you look at the green complex, one of the first features that will catch your eye is the green itself. Before you address your approach shot, see what you can determine about the green's size and shape. First, see if you can make a judgment about its surface size and two-dimensional shape. Next, determine its three-dimensional shape, that is, whether it's flat, convex, concave, or indefinite. Concave or bowled greens funnel approach shots toward the center of the green and are "friendly" to approach shots. Convex or crowned greens, on the other hand, are "unfriendly"

THE PAR-4 SEVENTEENTH HOLE AT ATLANTIC GOLF CLUB IN BRIDGEHAMPTON, NEW YORK, FEATURES CONTAINMENT MOUNDING AND ELABORATE BUNKERING DEFENDING THE APPROACH.

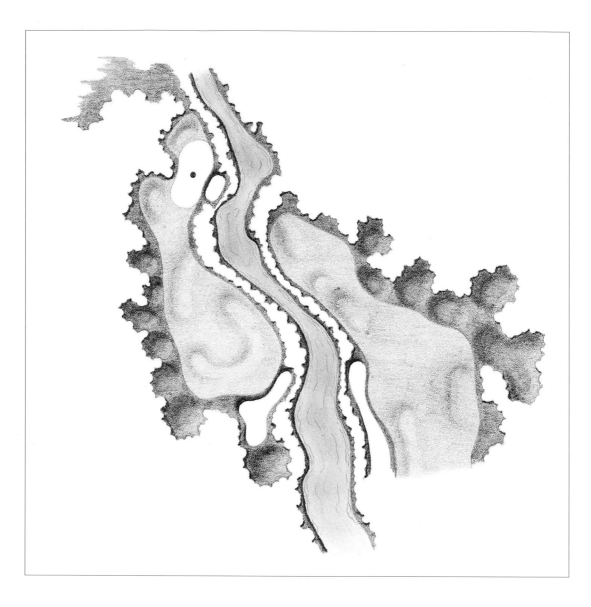

Swales and grassy hollows are often placed
near the putting surface but sometimes can be used in
landing areas as well on holes like the par-4
fifth at Prairie Landing Golf Club near Chicago, Illinois.

because approach shots tend to roll off them. Prime examples can be found on the Pinehurst No. 2 course in North Carolina designed by Donald Ross, who was renowned for his convex greens. If you are unfamiliar with a course, and the green's size and shape are not obvious at first glance, I suggest that you check the scorecard to see if it has a diagram of the green, walk around the landing area to get a better view (especially if a hill or mound provides a good vista), or ask your caddie.

Having determined the green's size and shape, carefully observe where the pin is located. Then decide where you want to land your approach shot given the pin's location and the green's shape and size.

Be aware that on downhill holes, the green is often hung on a fallaway slope, resulting in a difficult recovery if you overshoot it. Conversely, on uphill holes, the green is often pitched from back to front for improved visibility, and shots that carry too far may require you to negotiate a tricky downhill chip or pitch.

Designers frequently incorporate mounds or slopes into the green complex. They may be friendly, defensive, or even penal, so whenever you detect a mound or slope, determine whether it can help you get close to the flagstick and factor this knowledge into your shot selection. Also be aware that some mounds will be completely out of play for a certain shot but may be important with a different flagstick location or angle of approach. While slopes in the green complex may deflect a ball away from the putting surface, they may also be used to work a shot into a particular pin position. When studying a mound or slope, always consider the severity or degree of tilt to determine how the ball will react when it lands. Generally, the greater the tilt, the larger the effect, and the more the ball will move when it deflects off the mound or slope.

Other elements that can be blended into the green complex are swales and grassy hollows. Designers generally utilize these features

U.S. Open venues like Hazeltine National Golf Club in Chaska, Minnesota, site of the 1970 and 1991 championships, are synonymous with deep rough.

to create surface drainage and to test your ability to execute different recovery shots. Because drainage is one of the most important issues that golf course designers deal with today, oftentimes a swale or grassy hollow contains a catch basin or drain for capturing water runoff.

Swales tend to be shallower than grassy hollows, and grass height can be maintained as either fairway or rough depending on the shot options the designer wants to create. In those instances where the grass is maintained at fairway height, you are presented with a variety of shot-making choices — for example, a chip, a pitch-and-run, a bump-and-run, or even a putt — so shot selection can be just as important as execution. If the grass is maintained as rough, you are normally required to pitch or lob the ball out.

Grassy hollows, on the other hand, are usually fairly deep and may partially obstruct your view of the putting surface or bottom of the flagstick. These areas are almost always maintained at rough height, limiting recovery options to lofted shots. The slopes on grassy hollows can be steep. When in doubt, opt for a safe escape rather than a daring recovery.

The fringe, or collar, surrounding the putting surface is an important feature. This small section of turf grass, normally two to three feet wide, can have a major effect on shorter approach shots. When playing from bunkers or rough near the green, you are often forced to land the ball in this area to get it close to the hole. The fringe condition varies significantly depending on maintenance practices. Height, texture, and condition of the grass become extremely important. The best way to tell what confronts you is to closely survey the area itself and walk on the collar. Use your feet to ascertain the degree of firmness.

Finally, an often overlooked but critical feature of the green complex is the presence and character of rough, because it largely dictates the types of shot you can play there. Generally speaking, the lower or tighter the grass is manicured, the greater the opportunity to keep the ball low to the ground by running, chipping, or putting. The longer the grass, the more you will need to elevate the ball by pitching, lofting, or lobbing it. Be sure to take this factor into account before you select your shot.

Take the length of the rough during the U.S. Open Championship, which the USGA specifies to be heavy and deep. As a consequence, the chip, the pitch-and-run, and the bump-and-run are essentially eliminated and other shots are rendered treacherous — as Taiwan's Chen Tze-Chung can attest. During the 1985 U.S. Open at Oakland Hills Country Club in Birmingham, Michigan, "T.C." was enjoying a three-stroke lead when his approach shot got hung up in the deep, tangly rough grass surrounding the fifth green. While making a long, deliberate swing, T.C.'s club slipped under the ball, causing him to double-hit it. He staggered away with a quadruple-bogey and wound up losing the tournament by one stroke.

ON THE PAR-4 NINTH HOLE AT WISLEY GOLF CLUB'S MILL NINE, A FAIRWAY-TO-GREEN TIE-IN PROVIDES PLAYERS WITH ALTERNATIVES FOR REACHING THE PUTTING SURFACE.

You should always identify the type of green entrance facing you because it will play a large part in determining the shots that will get you on the green. For instance, an open entrance will allow you to bounce the ball onto the green, which is unlikely with other entrance types.

The first type of green entrance is the basic fairway-to-green tie-in where the fairway connects directly into the putting surface. Normally, there is little or no elevation change. This entrance is commonly used when a lengthy approach shot is required, because it provides options to bounce, roll, pitch, bump and run, chip, or putt the ball onto the green.

Take a look at the photo of the 433-yard par-4 ninth hole at the Wisley Golf Club's Mill Nine. Notice how the putting surface connects with the fairway and almost becomes an extension of it. Here you can either fly or bounce the ball onto the green.

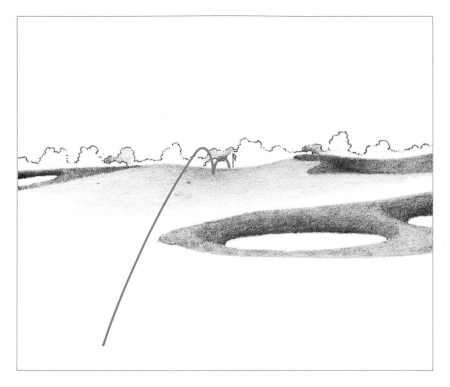

A ramp allows golfers a chance to bounce their ball onto the green on the par-4 ninth hole at The Orchards Golf Club near Detroit, Michigan.

Designers vary the width of a green entrance depending on the length of the approach shot. For longer approaches, the entrance area may be as wide as the green itself. Conversely, with a short approach you may encounter an entrance that's only half the width of a green.

Another type of entrance area is the *runway* or *ramp.* Usually this is a narrow strip of land, maintained at fairway height, that sweeps up between a pair of bunkers or other features to a green that is elevated to some degree. Because the ramp is always narrower than the width of the green, successfully bouncing the ball into the green requires extreme accuracy. Another factor that restricts the run-up option is the elevation change, which will slow or stop an approach shot. This type of entrance is usually used only by players who cannot fly the ball to the putting surface. When you encounter a ramp, you should understand that the designer

intended you to attack the green in an aerial manner and use the runway only as a last resort.

Occasionally, designers create a small portion of fairway, almost always detached from the major fairway, that connects with the green's front edge. This type of entrance area, known as a *tongue*, is usually defined by rough on its perimeter. A tongued area is normally employed to show golfers an acceptable entrance to the green and to give them an area in which to land the ball short and roll it onto the putting surface. Like the ramp, the tongue generally represents a less desirable option for approaching the flag, but it may be the only way under certain conditions.

If you come to rest on a tongued area, you should consider playing a chip shot or putting. The putter can be an effective tool here, especially if the grass is tightly maintained and you are not facing any major elevation changes. If you are confronted by an elevation change, then a chip or pitch shot is the better choice. An important

AT CRYSTAL TREE'S PAR-3 FIFTEENTH, A PAIR OF TONGUED AREAS DELINEATE THE PROPER ENTRANCES TO THE PUTTING SURFACE.

point to remember when dealing with a tongued area is that lies tend to be tighter, increasing the possibility of mishitting a chip or pitch. When in doubt, opt for the putter.

Another entrance situation you may encounter, which is becoming more common in modern-day design, is what I call a side *angle tie-in*. Here the front portion of the green is closed with bunkers or other obstacles much in the same manner as in a forced carry situation. But, unlike a forced carry, an alternate route is created to the side of the green by looping a portion of the fairway around the obstacles, thus giving players another entry option.

Look at the illustration of the 510-yard par-5 seventh hole at Weston Hills Country Club in Fort Lauderdale, Florida, site of the PGA Honda Classic. A series of bunkers is positioned in front of the green, requiring golfers who want to play straight for the hole to attack it aerially. I have also routed a portion of the fairway around to the side and connected it to the right edge of the green, allowing players to play around the bunkers and reach the green. During the first round of the 1992 Honda Classic, PGA Tour player Fred Couples used this section of fairway to his advantage by playing his second shot to the right of the green. He then executed a marvelous bump-and-run shot to obtain his birdie. Like Couples, you should consider taking advantage of these areas when the opportunity presents itself.

You will also encounter situations where there is no entrance because the designer has cut off the front of the green with bunkers, rough, or other hazards, forcing you to carry the ball to the putting surface. These situations present no option other than selecting a club that will carry you safely over the trouble.

FINESSE SHOTS

There are several shots you will find extremely useful for attacking the flag. The first is the *full shot* from the fairway or rough. Short hitters in particular will have a greater need for this shot, which involves knowing the relative distances your various clubs travel and selecting the appropriate club for your final target. Expert players generally prefer a full shot to create maximum height and backspin for the purpose of stopping the ball quickly on the putting surface. As you get closer to the green, full shots are no longer possible and delicate finesse shots must be mastered.

The next type of shot that can be very effective for attacking the flag is the *pitch,* which is probably the most commonly used shot inside 100 yards because it embraces a wide variety of distances and trajectories. The pitch shot evolved out of the need to play the ball over obstacles that defended the green. Designers have contributed to the art of pitching by placing bunkers, water, and other hazards close to the green complex. Another advantage that the pitch provides is that it can be stopped reasonably quickly after it lands, but not as quickly as a full shot.

Another useful shot is the *punch shot,* a low trajectory shot used to combat wind. In theory, the punch shot will be executed to stay as close to the ground as possible, but just high enough to avoid any major obstacles that need to be carried.

The closer you get to the green, the more specialized the shot-making requirements become, and the more your decision about which shot to use becomes paramount to good scoring.

The most commonly used shot near the green is the *chip.* It can be used from the fairway or the rough area, assuming there is enough green available to allow the ball to run to the hole. A basic chip shot can be executed with anything from a 4-iron to a sand wedge. An ideal chip shot should barely carry onto the green and release toward the flag. Because a chip is normally executed within a few yards of the green's edge, you can expect this shot to originate from light rough, a swale, the collar, or an entrance area.

A well-executed chip shot should carry just onto the green, stay low to the ground, and roll naturally toward the hole.

Unlike the chip, a pitch shot lands, bounces, and runs a short distance toward its intended target.

Certain areas around the putting surface may require use of the bump-and-run, where you land the ball short of the green and let it feed to the hole.

The lob is the most delicate of the short game shots, requiring feel and imagination to get the ball close to the target.

CHIP

PITCH

LOB

BUMP AND RUN

The second most common green-side shot is the *short pitch*. Under normal circumstances, it can be played from a variety of locations. In contrast to the low, running character of a chip shot, the short pitch is always played with a pitching wedge or sand wedge into the air for the purpose of avoiding an obstacle between you and the hole. The short pitch can be executed from either fairway or rough and produces a ball that lands more softly than a chip and stops reasonably well.

Another useful weapon in the vicinity of the green is the *bump-and-run*. Basically, the bump-and-run is a shot that lands short of the green and utilizes the slopes and contours to help the ball work its way toward the hole. Through the incorporation of chipping areas, entrance areas, swales maintained at fairway height, and other well-manicured features, designers frequently create opportunities to play the bump-and-run around greens as a means of testing a player's feel and touch. The trick is in determining how hard to hit the shot, where to land the ball, and how far the ball will roll.

The fourth essential shot is the *lob*, which can be played from almost anywhere around the green — from deep rough, a grassy hollow, or a manicured fairway well below a green's surface. It is almost always played with a sand wedge and basically involves putting as much height on the shot as needed to make the ball land softly and stop near the hole. The lob, also known as a *flop shot*, is the best way to deal with greenside defenses that require a short carry, such as a deep bunker or a water hazard. It is also useful in negotiating major slopes and undulations on the putting surface itself.

An often overlooked yet extremely useful shot from just off the green is the *Texas wedge*. Played with a putter, this shot can be executed from the fringe, an entrance area, a bunker with no lip or face, or even the light rough around the putting surface. The key to the Texas wedge is that it can provide better distance control in many situations just off the putting surface, and there is less risk of mishitting it than a short pitch or chip. For most beginner and intermediate players, the Texas wedge is easier to execute than other recovery shots, especially if your lie is bare, tight, or less than perfect.

When you are close to the green, identifying and understanding the countless ways designers set up the green complex will help you choose the right shot for each situation. To maximize results, you must also learn to select the proper club. While you can use many different clubs to execute the above shots, the wedges will usually be your best choice.

Know Your Wedges

Most golfers traditionally carried two wedges until the mid-1980s: a pitching wedge and a sand wedge. Because of recent innovations in golf course design, some lower-handicap players and professionals now carry three wedges to combat difficult lies and severe hazards in the green complex. Additionally, the three-wedge system will simplify club selection inside 100 yards.

Although there are various types of wedges that perform different functions, this discussion will focus on the following three basic wedges: the pitching wedge, the sand wedge, and the "lob" or "L" wedge. The more you understand about them, the better chance you have of getting the ball close to the hole.

The key characteristics of a wedge are loft, weight, and bounce. Loft refers to the face's angle with respect to the ground. This angle determines the height and length of the shot; weight will have a bearing on resistance to turf or sand; and bounce refers to how readily the club will dig into or skid off turf or sand. The width of the club sole determines bounce. Bounce increases as the width of the club's sole increases. The greater the bounce, the more a club will skid or resist penetrating into turf, soil, or sand. Clubs with little bounce will dig deeper into grass, soil, or sand.

You should choose your wedges on the basis of where you play most of your golf. Generally, there are three factors to consider: (1) texture and depth of sand, (2) thickness of fairways and roughs, and (3) soil conditions. On courses featuring firm conditions and tight lies, you should consider using wedges with less bounce and weight; on courses with softer conditions and heavier lies, wedges with more bounce and weight may assist you in dealing with the ground's resistance to the head of the club. If you play in different environments or geographical locations, you should give some thought to having two sets of wedges. Most expert players have a closet full of wedges that they can choose from to meet the conditions they face.

The pitching wedge has the least loft of the three wedges (usually between 48 and 53 degrees, with a standard loft of 50 degrees), and can be struck the farthest. Compared with the other two wedges, it has less bounce. The pitching wedge is normally used for full shots from the fairway, longer pitch shots, punch shots, and pitch-and-run shots. It can also be used to execute difficult long bunker shots (30 to 100 yards). Because of its reduced loft, it imparts less spin than sand or lob wedges, so expect the ball to run more when it lands.

Prior to the development of the sand wedge by golfing legend Gene Sarazen in the 1930s, sand bunkers constituted formidable hazards even for expert players. Through experimentation with different types of bunker shots, Sarazen found the amount of bounce that worked most effectively.

Although many golfers don't fully appreciate its virtues, the sand wedge may be the most versatile and useful club in a golfer's arsenal. Its loft usually runs between 53 and 60 degrees (with a standard loft of 55 or 56 degrees). Because of the substantial loft,

TOM WATSON WILL FOREVER BE REMEMBERED
FOR HIS DRAMATIC CHIP-IN AT THE PAR-3
SEVENTEENTH HOLE DURING THE FINAL ROUND OF
THE 1982 U.S. OPEN AT PEBBLE BEACH.

most players will be able to hit the sand wedge only a short distance. It can be used to execute a multitude of shots in many situations in and around the green complex, including pitches, short pitches, chips, lobs, and bunker "explosion" shots. Skilled players sometimes use a sand wedge to putt (blade) the ball when it is resting against the first cut of rough. The selection of a sand wedge suited to your game is paramount to your chances for short-game success.

The third type of wedge evolved over the past decade and is known as the "lob" or "L" wedge. This specialty wedge has a very high degree of loft, from 60 to 65 degrees (standard loft is 60 degrees), and it is used for hitting a high trajectory or lob shot that lands softly. It can be used for a recovery shot from behind a bunker to a green with the pin tucked tightly to the bunker. This wedge is particularly useful on courses where the design emphasizes sharp elevation changes and deep bunkers around the greens, or on courses with thick, heavy rough and fast greens. More and more, today's pros carry this club for such situations, especially in major championships.

In recent years, several major tournaments have been decided by spectacular short-game shots. In the 1981 U.S. Amateur Championship at the Olympic Club, Nathaniel Crosby, son of the late crooner Bing Crosby, rolled in a 25-foot birdie putt from the fringe with a Texas wedge to capture the title; in the 1983 Hawaiian Open, Isao Aoki of Japan holed out a long wedge shot on the eighteenth hole for an eagle to win the tournament; in the 1986 PGA Championship, Bob Tway sank a short bunker shot to stun Greg Norman; in the 1987 Masters, Larry Mize holed a 140-foot bump-and-run shot to shock the hard-luck Norman again; in the 1992 Bob Hope Desert Classic, John Cook chipped in on successive holes to defeat Gene Sauers; and in the 1992 U.S. Open, Tom Kite sank a lob shot from heavy rough at the par-3 seventh hole at Pebble Beach that propelled him to victory.

Probably the most compelling evidence of the short game's importance in deciding a major event occurred in the 1982 U.S. Open Championship at Pebble Beach: golfing great Tom Watson will be forever remembered for his dramatic chip-in birdie from the thick rough bordering the 218-yard par-3 seventeenth hole. Many people may have forgotten that Watson also saved par from heavy rough below the 436-yard par 4 tenth green and holed a Texas wedge from the fringe at the 555-yard par-5 fourteenth hole. Watson's short-game wizardry catapulted him to victory.

These dramatic successes underscore the importance of conquering the green complex. The more proficient you become in maneuvering the ball to the hole, the easier time you will have dealing with the greens, the subject of the next chapter.

Regardless of how flat a green may appear, every putting surface contains minor amounts of break.

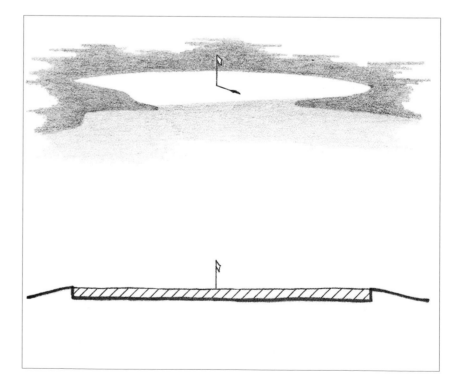

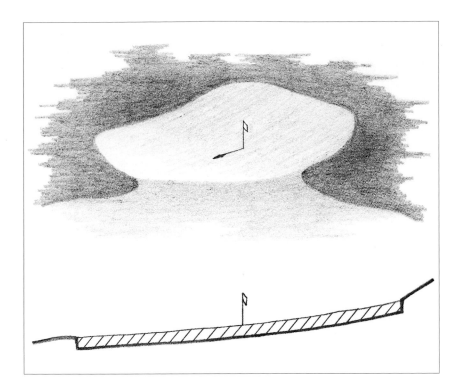

Sloped greens have gradual amounts of elevation change in their design.

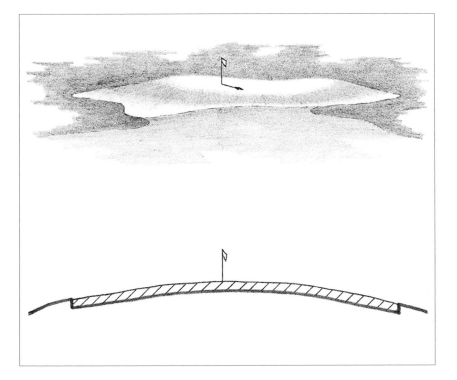

Pinpoint accuracy is necessary when approaching a crowned green because shots tend to fall away from the center.

Bowled greens are more receptive, because approach shots usually gather toward the middle.

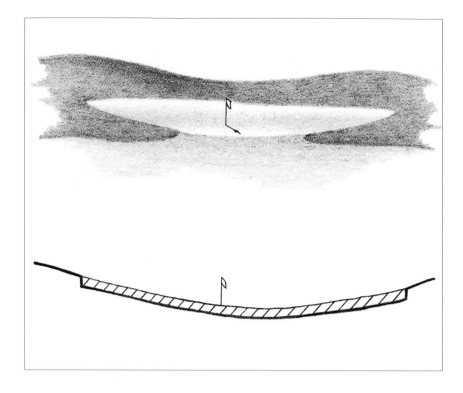

On decked greens, if you fail to position your ball on the proper level, a difficult putt will result.

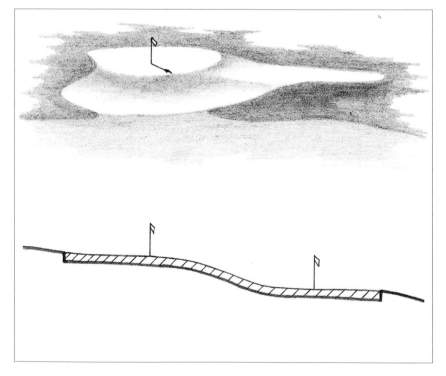

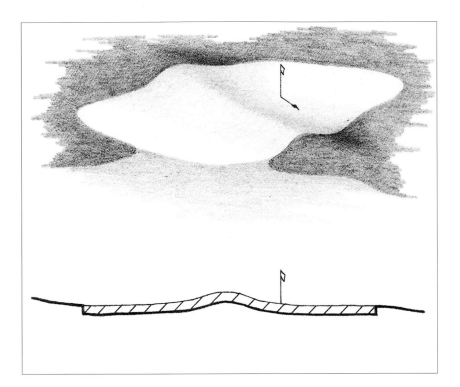

When analyzing up-and-over greens, careful evaluation of the area beyond the transition is essential for short-game success.

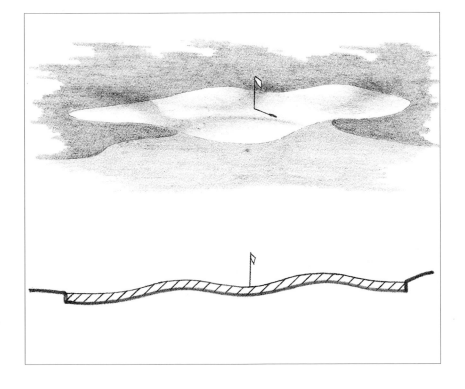

Contoured and rolling greens require accurate approaches and present difficult putting challenges.

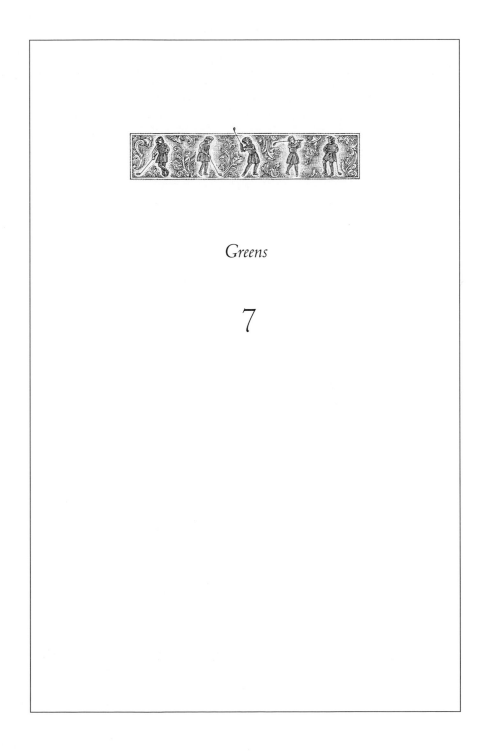

Greens

7

An example of an early square
green is the par-4 fifth hole at Crail
Golf Club near St. Andrews.

Preceding Page:
The green on the par-3 sixteenth hole at
Spanish Bay is divided by a hogback,
making putting an adventure.

In the early days of golf, the entire course was played in its natural state, so there were no greens as we know them today. The pin area was indistinguishable from the surrounding terrain. Only in the late 1800s did mowing and other maintenance equipment develop to such an extent that greenskeepers could maintain greens to a standard that clearly differentiated them from the rest of the course. Designers continued to position greens in areas with natural green characteristics, and sometimes they were laid out simply by pacing off a square of roughly 30 paces by 30 paces, which is about the area of an average modern green. In the photo, you can see a good example of a square green found on the fifth hole at the Crail Golf Club near St. Andrews. About the start of the twentieth century, designers began using earth-moving techniques to form and contour greens, and, as golf moved inland away from the windy links sites, elevated greens were created to facilitate drainage and putting surfaces tended to become smaller.

From the early 1900s to about 1930, greens design and shaping evolved rapidly thanks to the work of Ross, Tillinghast, Mackenzie, Macdonald, and others. The incorporation of contours into the green truly became an art form. In the post–World War II period, Dick Wilson and my father continued this evolution through their designs of large, sweeping greens with two or more distinct pinning areas. In the late 1950s and 1960s, the popularization of professional golf led to the creation of smaller greens to challenge the pros' shot-making abilities.

The golf boom that began in the 1970s and continues today introduced a new consideration — the tremendous increase in the number of rounds being played on many courses. Some designers resumed creating larger greens to provide more pin positions, allowing surfaces to remain in good shape despite the greatly increased traffic. During this period, contour creation intensified, sometimes producing overly detailed greens. The last few years have seen a movement back toward less contoured putting surfaces.

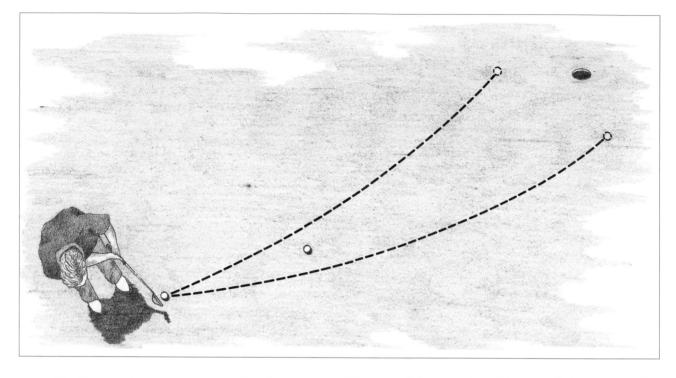

The old stymie rule made for imaginative shot making and rewarded players who maneuvered their ball close to the hole.

In short, greens, like snowflakes, are found in an infinite variety of sizes and shapes. They are limited only by the architect's imagination.

Once you are close to or on the putting surface, there is a tendency to breathe a sigh of relief because the difficult part is behind you. Remember, though, that while this is certainly true from a physical point of view, the quest for your best score is far from over. Golf consists of two games: (1) getting the ball from the tee to the green and (2) holing it. While the two games require very different skills, at least today you won't find yourself stymied on the green.

Match play in professional tournaments was prevalent until the 1950s, and you were said to be stymied when you had to putt with your opponent's ball lying in your line to the hole. The obstructing ball could be lifted only if it were within six inches of your ball. That's why scorecards used in club competitions were exactly six inches across — to measure for the occasion. Although the word "stymie" never appeared in the Rules of Golf, the stymie rule

gave rise to some devilish playing situations, as well as fabled
stories of players lofting their balls over their opponent's balls to
negotiate stymies. The rule was changed in 1951 to require all
obstructing balls to be marked and lifted. Today stymies exist mainly
in our heads — which doesn't make them any easier to overcome.

From a scoring point of view, the "second game" is just as important
as the first when you consider that golfers of all playing levels take
about half their shots on or around the green. While these shots are
short, success is not easily achieved. Strokes are gained or lost on
the green as they are nowhere else. When you sink a long putt, you
pick up one or even two strokes. On the other hand, a minor miscalculation on a short putt results in a stroke that is irretrievably
lost. There is no recovery possibility, miraculous or otherwise, that
can recapture it.

The results of a study published in 1989 underscore the rigors of
the second game. According to it, PGA Tour players sink only
54.8 percent of their six-foot putts and 83.1 percent of their three-
footers. Not surprisingly, the study also shows that amateurs sink

considerably lower percentages, so an excellent opportunity exists to lower your score if you can improve your second game by learning more about the green.

As you prepare for a shot near or on the green, your principal concerns will be contour and speed. Contour refers to the slopes, undulations, and other three-dimensional features of the putting surface. A green's contours do not change, although the pin position and the location of your ball will determine which specific contours will concern you. Speed is largely related to turf conditions (the height of the cut, whether it's lush or sparse, wet or dry, the grass variety, etc.) and can vary noticeably even during the same day.

When you are off the green, you will usually be concentrating on positioning your ball close to the hole rather than sinking it. Your lie, distance from the green, and elevation probably make several shots and clubs possibilities. Major contour features and overall speed conditions will be of greatest interest because the shot chosen will not be as delicate as a putt started on the green.

When you're on the green, you are executing the game's most delicate shot, which is to try to sink the ball or get it very near the hole, and you will be concerned with subtle contour and speed features that may affect its path. The playing conditions are relatively ideal: your lie is excellent; there is no grass, sand, or other material to interfere with ball-club contact; and the ball's entire journey will be over the most manicured part of the golf course. As on the tee, the Rules allow you to control some important playing conditions. For example, you will often see professionals mark a ball, pick it up, inspect it for damage (and, with a competitor's approval, substitute a new ball if it was cut or scraped during the prior shot), clean it, and, when replacing it, align its markings along the line of the putt to help their aim.

Whether you are close to or on the green, look for overall slope and drainage patterns in the putting surface as well as around the

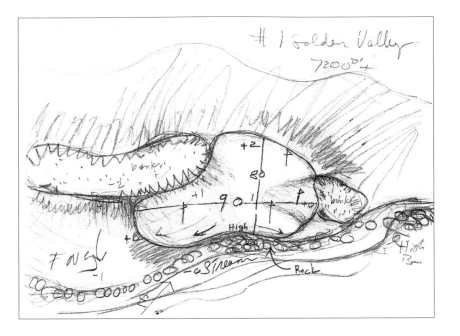

green itself. You will find that many greens drain rainfall off the surface in three different directions, which can give rise to subtle but important contours.

SIZE

The green's size often provides a preview of its contours. If it's small, expect mild contours. A larger green, on the other hand, likely presents more and stronger contours.

When you look at a large green, see if it really consists of two or more "component greens" that happen to be attached together. This "green comprised of smaller greens" configuration is not uncommon. Recognizing it will allow you to identify which of the component greens houses the pin. This is important because ending up on the wrong smaller green significantly increases your chances of three-putting or worse.

A good example appears in the sketch of the first green at the Golden Valley Golf Club in Hyōgo Prefecture, Japan. The large,

strongly contoured putting surface contains three smaller greens where the pin can be located. There are two small decks separated by a swale and a pair of substantial undulations that make it vital to be on the component green where the flag is located.

Although relatively rare on Scottish courses, the Old Course at St. Andrews features a number of double greens. Today's golf architects occasionally use this configuration, like those at the Golf Club de Genève in Switzerland and at The National Golf Club in Cape Schanck, Australia. So don't be surprised if you see two flags on a green. Just make sure you're aiming for the right one.

CONTOURS

Successfully attacking the pin from a position on the green or just off it requires an understanding of the contour features you will encounter. Contour features come in a virtually limitless variety of shapes and sizes. The following are some common contour

200

features found in the putting surface: slopes, decks, undulations, bowls, swales, humps, mounds, ridges, and hogbacks.

Slope is the most commonly found feature on a green surface. Every green has some slope, whether it be slight, gradual, or strong. Slope can be fairly uniform throughout an entire green or can vary substantially. The most important factor is the degree of tilt. The best way to picture a slope's profile is to visualize how water would flow if it were poured on the sloped area.

A deck is a relatively flat area where the hole can be placed. Elevation changes connecting flat areas produce decks in a green. Decks have minor amounts of slope as opposed to the stronger slopes that separate one deck from another. If you are positioned on the deck where the hole is located, expect a short to medium-length putt with less break. If you must traverse a stronger slope to reach a deck, it is important to examine both the stronger slope and the characteristics of the adjoining deck.

An undulation is an area containing several elevation changes in wavelike form. Decks are often connected by strong slopes or undulations. Some greens manifest undulation throughout without any discernible flat areas. Undulations often are difficult to analyze because they can combine multiple changes in the degree of slope affecting both the distance and the direction of a putt.

A bowl is simply a depression in the green whose sides usually contain moderate to strong degrees of slope. A putt entering a bowl from another portion of the green must allow for the increased speed gained from the bowl's downslope. Conversely, when putting out of a bowl, you must strike the ball with enough force to negotiate the bowl's incline. Bowls are generally designed to contain pinnable areas in the lower positions.

A swale is a low-lying, meandering, channel-type area, usually with a fairly gentle degree of slope. It is easy to overlook the subtle

When you are confronted with contours,
carefully examine features near the pin to
determine how the putt will react.

nature of this less intense contour feature. Swales generally slope toward the edge of the green to facilitate surface drainage and usually are not pinnable areas.

Finally, there are humps, mounds, ridges, and hogbacks. These convex contour features differ in size, style, and intensity. When they lie in your intended putting line, the required analysis is complex because you have to reckon with the effects of their uphill, downhill, and sidehill slopes.

When confronting any of these contour features, there is no substitute for knowledge gained through experience. You should practice with as many of these features as you can while carefully observing their effects on your shots in order to develop a feel for playing them.

If you are just off the green, you should consider the contour situation in making your club and shot selection, also taking into account pin placement. This may cause you to make a shot selection you would not otherwise make. For example, imagine you are about to chip to a green with a large undulation when you notice that the pin is above the undulation and the bottom of the undulation's incline is closest to you. Whereas normally you would chip the ball, this undulation could cause you to select a club and a shot that would allow you to lob the ball over it onto the flat area, avoiding the unpredictable effects the undulation could have on a chip.

On longer shots, besides studying the contour features between your ball and the pin, you may find it useful to observe the contour features immediately around and beyond the pin. For example, suppose you have a long uphill putt through a strong undulation and the pin is positioned so that if your shot overshoots it by 5 feet you will roll down the face of a slope and end up 15 feet from the pin facing a difficult uphill putt back to the hole. Many golfers will be so preoccupied with the undulation that they won't

THE BEFORE AND AFTER PHOTOS
OF THE PAR-3 SEVENTH HOLE AT PEBBLE
BEACH DEMONSTRATE THAT GREEN
SURFACES ARE OFTEN REFINED
OVER THE YEARS.

examine the area around and beyond the pin. A quick peek here might prompt you to play just short of the hole, leaving yourself, at worst, an easy second putt.

Frequently, during a round you can observe other greens prior to encountering them and gain valuable information about pin placement and contours. Be certain to capitalize on this useful yet often overlooked opportunity.

Speed

"Speed" refers to how quickly a ball will slow down on a flat area of a green. Technically, it is expressed in terms of readings on a Stimpmeter — a device George Stimp invented for the United States Golf Association. It is a metal device grooved to allow a golf ball to roll down its three-foot length onto a flat portion of a green. Traditionally, a slow green registers fewer than 7.5 feet of roll, a medium green 7.5 to 10.0, and a fast green more than 10.0.

Unfortunately, stimp readings generally are of little use. No one at a course, except perhaps the golf course superintendent, ever seems to know what the stimp reading is; factors like wind, sun, temperature, and rain can cause it to change rapidly; and even if you miraculously obtain an accurate stimp reading, it probably won't help you, because you must develop your own feel about whether a green is fast, slow, or medium.

The golf course superintendent largely establishes speed through maintenance practices. Mowing and irrigation are but two of the operations under the superintendent's control that dramatically affect speed. If the greens are cut low on a given day, they will be faster than if they were cut higher. Irrigation directly affects speed by producing a lusher or leaner stand of grass, as well as a firmer or softer surface. Weather, too, influences speed. Rain, fog, and early-morning dew provide moisture, which decreases speed; as the grass dries, speed picks up.

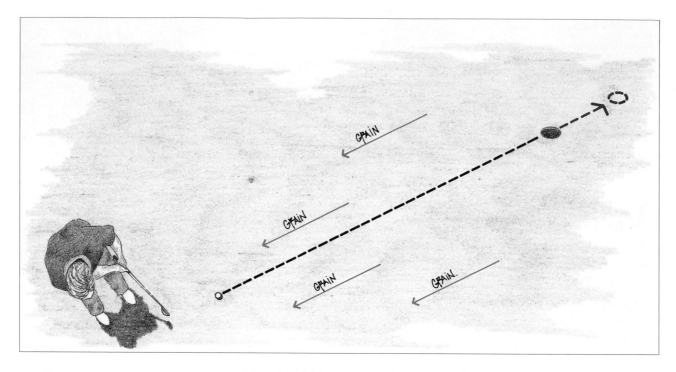

When putting against the grain, strike the ball a little harder to compensate for the resistance of the grass.

You should be aware of two related grass properties that affect speed: grain and resistance. Grass has grain if the blades grow in a relatively horizontal fashion with respect to the putting surface. Resistance refers to how quickly grass on a putting surface will slow down a ball, and it depends on a number of factors, including grain, height, quality, and grass type.

The effects of grain are easily understood by looking at several hypothetical examples. Assume that you have a level 10-foot putt on a bermudagrass green with no grain. After several attempts, you master the speed needed for your ball to roll exactly into the center of the cup. Now, imagine the only difference is that the grain runs toward you; that is, each blade grows relatively horizontally in your direction. To reach the center of the cup, you will have to stroke the ball harder. If the grain runs away from you, you can hit a considerably softer putt and still reach the hole.

Grain can run in any direction with respect to the line of your putt. Once you have identified its direction, you can easily forecast its general effect on your shot. The problem is that it's often very difficult to determine exactly how the grain runs and the intensity of its effect. The results of a putting machine experiment emphasized the unpredictable nature of grain.

The experiment involved a machine called a Tru Roller, which produced putts that would roll in the ideal direction every time and could be set to roll the ball at the ideal speed. When it hit several putts from the same spot 12 feet from the hole, the balls wore a delicate path to the hole, producing a uniform consistency in the grain that resulted in putts that almost never missed. But when the path was brushed away after each putt and the grain was restored, the Tru Roller could sink the putt only about 70 percent of the time, confirming what many observant expert golfers know: grain is frequently a critical factor in determining a putt's path and final

PINE LAKE GOLF CLUB WAS THE FIRST COURSE IN THE KANSAI REGION OF JAPAN TO DEVELOP A SINGLE BENTGRASS GREEN, NOW THE NORM IN THIS AREA.

Observing the roll and break of putts by your playing partners can help you obtain a better feel for the greens.

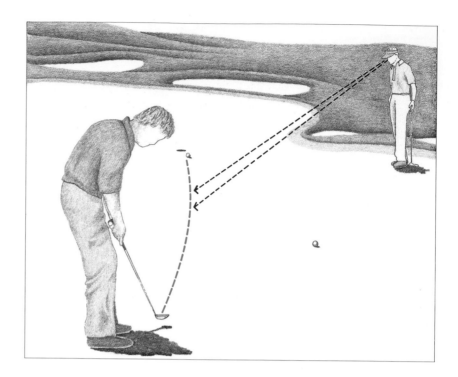

destination. Grain may be a large reason PGA Tour players make only 54.8 percent of their six-foot putts.

The only way to develop a feel for the effect of grain is through experimentation and practice. Don't be surprised, though, if a particular green has no discernible grain or if the grain runs in different directions. Many greens have these characteristics.

There are several ways to determine grain direction, but none is foolproof. Probably the best way is to look at the edge of the hole. If one side has a thin strip of soil and the opposite side has grass growing over it, the grain almost certainly runs from the grassy side to the soil side. Common lore also has it that grain runs toward the setting sun, away from mountains, and in the same direction that water drains from the putting surface. Finally, color and shade can offer you a clue. A dull, gray appearance indicates that the grain runs away from you, and a shiny, darker look indicates that it runs toward you.

Climate is the principal factor determining the grass type you can expect to encounter. In some climate areas, seasonal changes are handled by overseeding or even the use of a two-green system, as has been done in Japan and Korea. In the two-green system, one green generally consists of bentgrass for cool-season play and the other of korai for warmer periods. Today, however, because of improvements in turf grass and agronomic techniques, few new courses use this system.

The following grass types frequently are used on greens. I have noted some of their important characteristics that can affect play on the green. If you're not sure about the grass type, ask the pro, superintendent, or another staff member.

Bentgrass is one of the most commonly used grass types for greens in cool or temperate climates. Frequently, it has little grain due to its upright growth habit, and its resistance is low thanks to its fine leaf blades. Because this grass can be cut and easily maintained at very low heights, bentgrass greens often are fast.

Bermudagrass is a warm-season grass with coarser leaf blades than bentgrass. It is frequently found on greens in warmer climates, grows quickly, and offers moderate to high resistance. Almost invariably, it has noticeable grain due to its horizontal growth propensity. When bermudagrass is maintained at low heights, grain becomes less of a factor and speed increases dramatically. Because bermudagrass is harder to maintain at low heights than bentgrass, anticipate that bermuda greens may be slower than bentgrass greens. In predominantly bermudagrass regions (that is, hot, humid areas like the tropics and southeastern U.S.) designers tend to incorporate more intense contour features into greens because of the grass's normally slower speeds.

Fine fescue is a cool-season grass with thin blades, a bristly feel, and moderate to strong resistance. It usually lacks a prevailing grain direction because it grows in groups of individual plants whose blades develop in a sporadic manner. Normally maintained at moderate heights, it cannot be maintained consistently as low as bentgrass, so greens that contain fine fescue are generally slower.

Annual bluegrass (usually called poa annua or poa) is a cool-season grass with strongly invasive characteristics in the presence of bent and fescue. Poa annua has a bushy, thatchy quality that is very pronounced when it is producing whitish seed heads. The poa annua leaves are usually a lighter shade of green than those of fescue or bentgrass. After cutting, it grows at a much faster rate than bent-grass or fescue and, because it's considerably taller, produces more resistance. When poa invades a putting green composed of other grasses, it generates a rough, bumpy surface that causes putts to deviate substantially from the path they could otherwise be expected to follow. Some course superintendents try to control or eliminate poa annua to avoid these "patchy" situations. Others — for example, at the Stanford University Course in California — try to maintain greens that are almost exclusively poa annua, which at least results in some consistency within the green surface.

Zoysia (also known as korai) is a warm-season grass often used on summer greens in Japan. Korai has thick, strong blades and a very high degree of resistance. It has pronounced grain characteristics that will strongly influence a shot. Korai goes dormant in the winter months and is used only on green surfaces during the warm season of the year.

Many greens, intentionally or unintentionally, mix two or more grass varieties that have very different grain and resistance character-istics. This happens with considerable frequency when poa annua invades bentgrass or fescue greens, because once poa annua estab-lishes itself, it grows at a much faster rate after mowing than bentgrass or fescue. These different growth rates produce variable grain and resistance scenarios for putts traveling through patches of different grasses. Recognizing and dealing with these patchy situations is extremely important, and you should carefully observe the various grasses between your ball and the hole and try to identify their grain and resistance qualities.

Ball Marks and Spike Marks

Ball marks are indentations in the putting surface made by approach shots. They become very important as you approach the hole because an unrepaired ball mark can make a ball bounce or roll off-line, causing you to miss a putt you might otherwise have made. The Rules of Golf allow you to repair ball marks anywhere on the green. These repairs should be done at every opportunity to increase your chances for putting success and to keep the green in top condition. Repairing a ball mark also gives you a good opportunity to learn something about the putting surface's firmness, which has a direct bearing on speed. The same type of information can be obtained by being sensitive to the sensations you get from your spikes as they enter the green surface.

Spike marks are scraped areas of turf grass caused by the spikes on the bottom of golf shoes. Spike holes and heel prints are closely related to spike marks. According to the Rules, they cannot be repaired along your line of play before your shot. The intensity of spike marks, spike holes, and heel prints increases the closer you get to the hole, and you should approach them as you approach grain or resistance: determine their effect on the path of your ball and adjust your speed and/or line accordingly.

Observe Shots on the Green

Observe how your approach shot reacts as it rolls across the green, especially as it passes near the hole. By watching a ball's entire journey, you can pick up useful information about contour and speed that may help you formulate your next shot. Likewise, take every opportunity to "go to school" by carefully observing the putts of other golfers as well as your own to gather data that you can use for your next shot. Keep in mind, however, when studying other golfers' approach shots and putts, the quality of the contact they make with the ball. A player may take a forceful stroke but mishit the shot, thereby distorting its informational value.

TIPS FOR PUTTS

Many of us probably had our first golfing experiences playing miniature golf. If anyone can grab a putter and tackle this game with no fear of making a fool of himself, why is the putter the most abused and accused club, and why does putting send legions of players to sports psychologists and other gurus? Perhaps it's because successfully executing this aspect of the game takes so little physical effort while requiring tremendous mental poise and concentration.

Late in his remarkable playing career, Ben Hogan still was striking the ball flawlessly from tee to green but was struggling mightily with his putting. Asked about this, Hogan replied, "Golf is one game, putting is quite another."

Players inevitably blame missed putts on their putters, which are justly punished for their transgressions. During the first round of the 1992 U.S. Open at Pebble Beach, PGA Tour player Ken Green noted that "my putter was acting up again." After finishing the round with three three-putt greens and one four-putt, he concluded, "I gave my putter its last rites, heaving it into the Pacific as far as I could. Usually I give my putters away, but this one was so horrible I could not wish it on anyone." Most of us probably have experienced similar emotions. The following are several putting tips that you may find useful.

On putts of more than 30 feet, your primary objective is to get the ball close to the hole. Initially, you'll need to determine how far your ball is from the cup, and the easiest way to do this is to pace

BEN CRENSHAW, ONE OF GOLF'S GREAT PUTTERS, BELIEVES THAT SPEED IS THE MOST IMPORTANT INGREDIENT FOR PUTTING SUCCESS.

off the distance according to the length of your stride. Next, get a feel for overall contour and speed features that your shot will encounter. You can do this by walking around the green to get views of your putt's path from the side as well as from behind your ball. Make sure that the line of your intended shot will leave you as close to the hole as possible. Now, strike the ball with the goal of ending up not more than a foot to 18 inches past the hole.

You will be well rewarded for spending time on the practice green developing a feel for these long putts. Golfers who have learned the distinct differences in feel between putts in 10-foot increments — that is, putts of 30, 40, 50, 60, etc., feet — have a tremendous advantage.

On putts shorter than 10 feet, your goal is to sink the ball, so your main concerns are subtle contours and speed. It is useful to bend down or crouch close to the ground over your ball to analyze subtle slopes around the hole, and you will see professionals making use of this technique. Medium-length putts require you to decide which of the various considerations you should emphasize.

From an architect's perspective, the putting surface is the most carefully detailed feature on a golf course. Designers expend great effort and time shaping and refining greens to obtain exactly the effects they desire. Each green presents different challenges and subtleties, which you can understand by applying the above principles. The act of putting is a different matter.

Putting is as individualistic as painting: everybody has a different stroke. The key is the finished product — getting the ball into the hole. There is no uniform blueprint for success. You have to find a putter and develop a style with which you are comfortable. Once you have these, it is crucial to clear your mind, be decisive, and focus on a single positive thought while standing over the ball, whether it be the specific line or the proper speed.

Ben Crenshaw, recognized as one of the game's great putters, has a simple philosophy for his success: "I don't have any big secret about putting," Crenshaw said, "I just hit at it. It's either going to miss or go in."

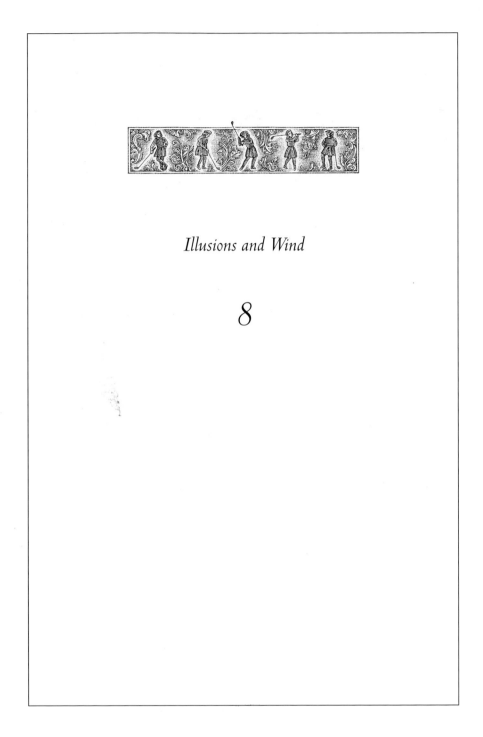

Illusions and Wind

8

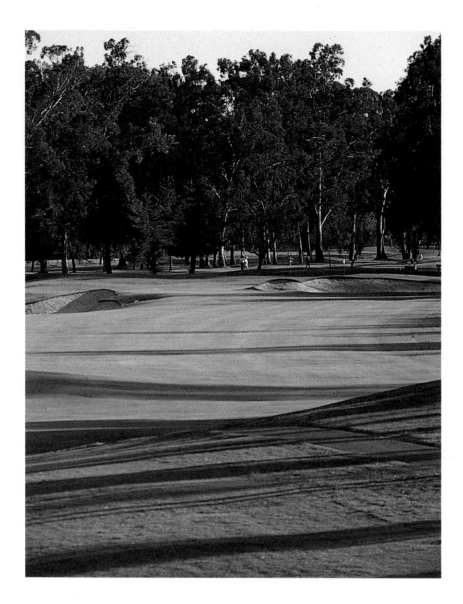

A HUGE FACE BUNKER CONCEALS THE LOCATION OF THE GREEN'S
FRONT EDGE AT RIVIERA COUNTRY CLUB'S PAR-4 THIRD HOLE, OFTEN
CAUSING GOLFERS TO MISJUDGE THEIR APPROACH.

PRECEDING PAGE:
THE PAR-4 TENTH HOLE AT ARROWHEAD GOLF COURSE IN ROXBOROUGH
PARK, COLORADO, FEATURES A GREEN SITUATED IN A VALLEY WITH MOUNTAINS
IN THE BACKGROUND, MAKING DISTANCE DIFFICULT TO DETERMINE.

During the 1990 U.S. Open at Medinah Country Club, I was walking the course when a friend asked, "Bob, see that bunker on the right side of the fairway — how far is it from the green?" I answered that the distance was about 30 yards. He turned to me astonished and said, "You've got to be kidding, it's flush against the putting surface, so there's no way it can be more than five yards." My friend was correct in that from where we stood in the fairway the bunker appeared to be guarding the edge of the green. As we approached the bunker, I explained the common technique the designer had used to create this illusion. Despite my explanation, it wasn't until we were almost next to the bunker that my friend realized that the distance really was about 30 yards.

This simple but effective technique involves building the bunker so that its far or top edge is visually aligned with the putting surface when viewed from the area where the approach shot is intended to be struck. The area between the bunker and the green is hidden, producing the illusion that the green and the bunker were close together. This illusion can cause golfers to underestimate the yardage and select an incorrect club.

Hiding an area in this way is one of the designer's favorite devices. It occurs in many situations, like fairways with swales or water hazards, and greens with decks. The objective is always the same: to create the illusion that the distance to your specific target is shorter (or occasionally greater) than actually is the case.

George Thomas was a virtuoso in the use of this technique, and some of his best work can be seen at the Riviera Country Club in Pacific Palisades, California, where he camouflaged large expanses between several greens surfaces and solitary, large, steep-faced bunkers. This distance dilemma at Riviera is compounded by the fact that the hidden expanses generally are swales of kikuyugrass, which inhibits bounce and roll. The third, fourth, twelfth, and

On Sta. Elena's par-3 fourteenth, the right side mound hides a bunker guarding the rear portion of the green from the golfer's view.

sixteenth holes are prime examples. During the annual Los Angeles Open, you will occasionally notice the PGA Tour players on these holes asking their caddies where their balls are, as they find it hard to believe that their shots did not reach the green.

The 155-yard par-3 fourteenth hole at our new Sta. Elena course near Manila is a wonderful example of this technique. It has two large mounds on opposite sides of the fairway, well short of the green, that create a narrow valley with a clear view of only the central portion of the green. The green appears to be directly behind the mounds, making it difficult to believe that the hole is really 155 yards in length.

An illusion is a misleading image presented to the eye — an image whose true physical characteristics are different than they appear. One powerful illusion with which everybody is familiar is the so-called moon illusion. A full moon at the horizon looks much larger than it does when it is higher in the sky even though the size of its image on the eye's retina is the same regardless of its position in the sky. Viewing the horizon moon through a cardboard tube it precisely fills, and thereafter viewing it higher in the sky, confirms this fact. Contrary to one popular misconception, the atmosphere does not magnify the image of the horizon moon.

Similarly, on the golf course, most illusions cause you to conclude that objects or areas are either closer or more distant than they really are. Now let's see why a golf course is such fertile ground for illusions.

Golf presents distance puzzles that make the game unique. Not only are we hitting the ball long distances while trying to place it in a relatively small area, but we are doing so without the benefit of a standardized playing field to help us determine yardages, as is the case with baseball, football, soccer, and other games. If there are no reference objects or guides, few, if any, golfers can look at an area and know whether it is 170, 180, or 200 yards away — differences of one to three clubs.

While our distance sense regarding relatively near objects depends importantly on having two eyes ("binocular vision"), cues for judging longer distances generally do not depend on binocular vision. As one scientist put it, for distances in excess of about 20 feet we are all effectively one-eyed ("monocular"), which we can prove to ourselves simply by closing one eye when viewing some far-off objects.

One of the primary monocular cues for judging distances is relative size. If we believe that distant objects, for example two trees, are the same size, we will judge the one that appears smaller to be farther away. Relative size is often used to create illusions on the golf course. Taller trees can be placed farther down the fairway than shorter trees. This can lead one to underestimate the relative distance between the taller and shorter trees and thus the actual distance to the taller trees.

*Bunkers, trees, and an open area behind the green make the
approach to the par-4 fifth hole at San Francisco Golf Club in
California appear shorter than actually is the case.*

Sometimes designers tempt you to focus on the near edge of a feature while ignoring the far, and critical, edge. To achieve this, the near portion is enlarged and made prominent while the distant portion is deemphasized or made less visible. Take a bunker on the corner of a dogleg that is intended to lure you into attempting to carry it to shorten the hole. The near side will be enlarged to get you to focus your attention on it while ignoring the far side. If this happens, you will probably underestimate the distance and end up in the bunker.

Designers can also create illusions by drawing your eye to dramatic features. The 166-yard par-3 sixteenth hole (the Flower Hole) at SentryWorld in Stevens Point, Wisconsin, is a good example. In the photo, you can see how we used brilliant flowers to focus the golfer's attention on the near edge of this feature. At other times, designers reverse the process to make the target area appear more distant than it really is by reducing a feature's size and positioning it close to the landing area.

On occasion designers use another ploy to discourage you from cutting a dogleg that you actually could cut without much trouble. A large bunker with a prominent face or other eye-catching feature is placed on the corner of the dogleg with its far edge raised to partially hide the landing area. If you improperly analyze this situation, you may take the longer route around the dogleg because you erroneously conclude that the landing area is narrower than it is. Because this device is used often, watch for it whenever there is a conspicuous feature in the dogleg that partially blocks your view of the landing area.

Often, a hole can be made to appear much longer than it really is by running alongside it a long, narrow feature like a bunker, waste area, or water hazard. Pete Dye is a master of this gambit. A good example of Dye's wizardry appears in the illustration of the 367-yard par-4 twelfth hole at his Mission Hills Dinah Shore Course in Palm Springs, California. In this case, the large expanse of water

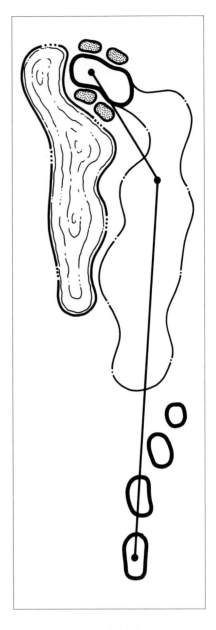

On the par-4 twelfth hole at Mission Hills' Dinah Shore Course, a long body of water makes the hole appear longer.

that skirts the left edge of the fairway stretches the hole out to the golfer's eye.

Trees, as we've already seen, can be used to produce a number of illusions. By placing them along both sides of a fairway, they can give the impression that the landing area is quite narrow even though the contrary may be true. Take our 470-yard downhill par-4 eighteenth hole at Golf Club de Grenoble in France. Stands of large trees line both sides of the start of this hole, but the trees on the left side stop about 200 yards from the championship tee, and, in reality, the landing area is wider than it appears from the tee.

Large trees also frequently induce you to hit short on your approach shot when they are positioned just off the back of the green. From a psychological point of view, players often become preoccupied with the prospect of playing out of trees, which causes them to underclub. In addition, if the trees are larger than the course's other trees or the trees you are used to seeing, they may make you think the green is considerably closer than it is. Mountains close to the back edge of greens can produce similar effects.

During my college days, I fell victim to this tree illusion during the NCAA Championship at Eugene Country Club in Eugene, Oregon. Being from New Jersey, I had never before played on a course with such gigantic trees — many of them positioned just off the back edge of greens. For most of the first round my approach shots were short. I adjusted my game when I finally convinced myself that these huge trees were fooling me into thinking that the greens were much closer than they actually were.

In this same vein, if you're not alert, flagstick heights can cause some heartburn regarding distance calculation. Heights vary considerably throughout the world — from seven feet in the United States to only five feet or so in coastal areas of the British Isles because of their strong winds. Nick Faldo has talked about the effort it takes for him to avoid underestimating yardages when he

THE PAR-3 SIXTEENTH HOLE AT SentryWorld FEATURES A CAPTIVATING FLOWER BED BETWEEN TEE AND GREEN, DRAWING YOUR ATTENTION TO THE FOREGROUND.

comes to the United States after having played in a string of
tournaments in Great Britain. On my British golfing excursions, I
have had to factor in the shorter flagsticks to keep myself from
overestimating yardages.

Complications in calculating distances that are caused by varying
tree and flagstick heights seem to validate my prior conclusion
about the difficulty of visually measuring distances. Perhaps no one,
not even Faldo, can eyeball a spot on the ground and feel confident
of its yardage without recourse to collateral reference guides like
trees or flagsticks.

Along these same lines, one of the most deceptive yardage-
calculating situations exists when a green is sited in an open area
devoid of reference objects. Our 334-yard par-4 eighth hole at
Poipu Bay Golf Resort, shown in the photo, is a good case in
point. Lacking reference guides, most players underestimate the
distance to the green and come up short. Underestimating distances

when there are no reference points may be attributable to the fact that we are not used to recognizing, in our daily lives, the differences between distances greater than 15 or 20 yards. I think players tend to underestimate distances because they are unaccustomed to consciously thinking, except on the golf course, of objects being as far away as 150 yards or more. Thus there seems to be a human propensity to think of objects as being closer than they really are.

Water hazards, which were discussed in Chapter 5, present this type of distance enigma, because they are flat and offer no reference markers. As a result they can also cause players to wind up short.

Players face a different type of illusion when the entire hole gradually ascends from tee to green. Because there are no sharp elevation breaks, many golfers underestimate the elevation change and finish up short of their targets. The long 441-yard par-4 thirteenth hole at Spyglass Hill provides an excellent example. Many players misjudge the magnitude of its steady, undramatic increase in elevation and underclub. The same occurs on Oak Hill's Hill of Fame 594-yard par-5 thirteenth hole in Rochester, New York, site of many U.S. Opens.

Radically descending holes also confront players with distance-gauging complications (as discussed in Chapter 2). The photograph shows the third hole on the Princeville Makai Course's Ocean Nine. This downhill par-3 over water presents golfers with the complex task of judging the actual distance the hole is playing. Although the scorecard indicates that it is 165 yards from the championship tee, it is safe to assume that the shot generally plays shorter because of the substantial drop. There are unusual days when there is a Kona headwind and the hole plays longer than the indicated yardage.

Golf folklore has it that greens in a mountain setting slope away from the mountain. Although this is possibly true, it is, I believe, an admonition to watch out for an illusion frequently encountered

in these settings. Because the overall landscape tends to flow downward away from the mountain, a green sloping in the same direction may appear flat. Likewise, a flat green may appear to slope toward the mountain.

These are just a few of the most common illusions you will encounter. Your own sensitivity to the fact that illusions are important facets of the game will prompt you to identify many more.

What's the best way to handle illusions? A good approach is to imagine that you are an expert pilot whose experience indicates the presence of an illusion. The pilot double-checks the cockpit instruments and, relying on them, sets and follows a flight plan. Adopting this approach to handling golf illusions, you rely on your "instruments" — yardage books, scorecards, route plans, distance markers, and the perspectives offered by different vantage points. For example, try walking over to the edge of a fairway, climbing a mound or nearby sideslope in the rough, or making your way to an elevated area near a bunker. A little extra survey work like this can take the mystery out of the areas ahead of you.

In support of the pilot analogy, a study of similar airplane crashes in the 1960s showed the power of misleading visual distance cues. In all cases, the planes approached airports over dark water on clear nights, and the runways had backgrounds of upward-sloping city lights. All the planes landed short of the runway, apparently because the pilots ignored their instruments and overestimated their altitudes. When these conditions were programmed into a flight simulator and experienced pilots attempted to land using only visual cues, almost all of them "crashed."

Weather and geographic conditions present another set of playing factors. We know that the ball carries farther at high altitudes than low ones. The same is true with respect to high and low temperatures and low and high levels of humidity. Generally,

WITHOUT A DISCERNIBLE BACKDROP, THE APPROACH SHOT TO THE PAR-4 EIGHTH HOLE AT POIPU BAY RESORT TENDS TO FEEL SHORTER THAN ITS TRUE DISTANCE.

though, wind is by far the most important of these factors, so let's examine this "invisible hazard" more closely.

Wind considerations play a material part in the design of many of my courses. When we start the design process, we carry out a thorough investigation of the site's prevailing, seasonal, and storm wind patterns. The results will influence how we route the course as well as how we configure certain features. If the prevailing wind blows from east to west, we will try to route the course so that fairway slopes will tend to minimize the prevailing wind's effect. We also might tip the greens from west to east to counteract the east-west prevailing wind. In like fashion, we would not normally route a 450 yard par-4 into the prevailing wind — it would play too long.

The design considerations are further complicated by the fact that windy sites often have seasonal and storm winds that blow in different directions than the prevailing wind. Our 172-yard par-3 twelfth hole at the Windsor Club in Vero Beach, Florida, was designed to take into account the prevailing and storm winds. The prevailing wind blows against you, quartering out of the left. The storm wind gusts from behind you, also quartering out of the left. To dampen the effects of these two winds, we designed the green to run from 8 o'clock to 2 o'clock with an open entrance area on its left side, as you can see in the following photo. On those rare occasions when the wind blows in a contrary fashion, say against you, quartering out of the right, this hole will present a formidable playing challenge that is the normal result with holes designed to accommodate the prevalent winds. Thus, on windy sites take extra care to determine if the wind is coming from an unusual direction, and if it is, factor it into your playing strategy.

Basically, there are four types of wind to be concerned about: tailwinds, headwinds, crosswinds, and quartering winds. Each will influence your shot in a different fashion.

A tailwind comes from behind you and blows in the general direction of your target. Spin on the ball will have less effect, and it will be difficult to shape your shots by fading or drawing them. A tailwind also generally causes your shot to carry farther, especially if you get extra loft on it.

A headwind blows directly toward you from your target and will amplify the effects of spin. Thus, a draw or fade will curve more than would otherwise be the case, and shots often will balloon, reducing carry. Consider using a less lofted club or playing the ball on a lower trajectory. Don't let a strong headwind intimidate you into overswinging.

A crosswind cuts across your shot line in a perpendicular fashion and will cause the ball to move right or left. The challenge here lies in gauging the wind's intensity and deciding how far right or left to start the shot so that the wind will push it to the target area.

A quartering wind blows toward you and cuts across your shot line at an angle. Under these circumstances, you will have to make both headwind and crosswind adjustments.

When playing in windy conditions, you should think about your next move as in chess or your "leave" as in pool. Ascertain how the wind will affect the way you play the shot following the one you are about to hit. This process may cause you to select a different shot than your initial impulse indicates. For example, if you are approaching a green defended by bunkers on the right side but "defenseless" on the left, the left normally would be the best place to miss the green because it presents the easiest recovery possibilities. If, however, there is a strong left-to-right crosswind, a recovery shot into the wind from a bunker on the right may be an easier shot, so your preferable "miss" area could be the right side.

When you are putting, you should also carefully observe wind conditions because a strong wind can substantially affect a putt's

The tee shot at the par-3 fourth hole at Cabo Real
Golf Club in Cabo San Lucas, Mexico, is difficult to judge
due to the horizon line in the background.

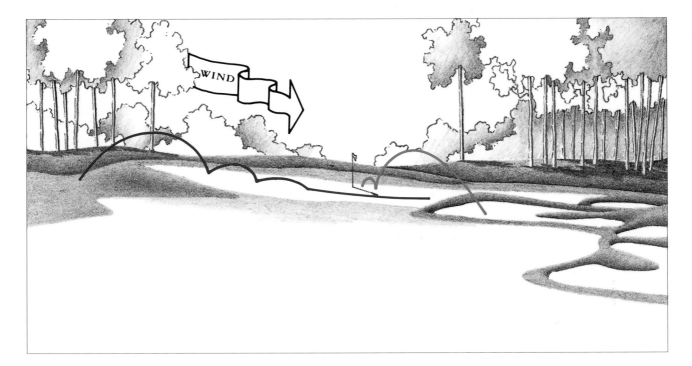

path. Experience and your sensitivity to this type of situation will enable you to develop putting touch and knowledge in windy conditions.

If you let it, wind will play havoc with your game. Remember, when you are playing in difficult wind conditions, everyone's score will go up. Have fun, raise par in your own mind, and remember the old and true maxim: "When it's breezy, swing easy."

In windy conditions, your best "leave" could be a bunker that might be considered difficult under normal circumstances.

AT THE PAR-3 THIRD HOLE ON THE PRINCEVILLE MAKAI'S OCEAN NINE, A VERTICAL DROP OF MORE THAN SEVENTY FEET CAN MAKE CLUB SELECTION CONFUSING.

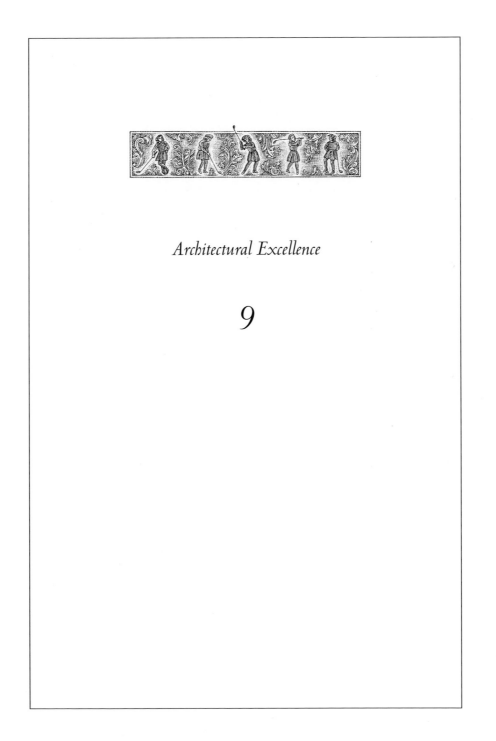

Architectural Excellence

9

IF YOU MISS THE GREEN OFF THE TEE ON
THE PAR-3 ELEVENTH HOLE AT ST. ANDREWS, YOUR
SHORT-GAME SKILLS WILL BE SEVERELY TESTED.

PRECEDING PAGE:
THE DOGLEG LEFT PAR-5 THIRTEENTH HOLE
AT AUGUSTA NATIONAL IS PLEASING TO THE EYE AND
SCORECARD, PROVIDED YOU AVOID RAE'S CREEK.

Now that we know the elements of scoring success, let's develop strategies for some classic holes that present intriguing golfing challenges. While the older holes are not identified with any particular architect, the modern selections are the offspring of the game's most prominent designers.

On occasion, writers and historians have tried to tag architects with overall styles, which, in my mind, is an impossible task. All of us have borrowed heavily from the venerated courses of the past, even if we have not done so consciously. The early American golf architects like Charles Blair Macdonald and Donald Ross drew extensively on what they had seen in the ancient United Kingdom courses. Moreover, a site's natural attributes frequently are so powerful that they essentially dictate the course's overall character. It is not unusual to come across two outstanding courses that even an expert in golf architecture would not perceive had been created by the same designer, because many accomplished designers share my philosophy of "listening to the land" and tailoring the course to it.

Let's embark on an imaginary tour of some of my favorite holes. We are out on the course enjoying its ambiance, formulating our strategy according to the conditions of the day. The sky is clear, the air is warm, and the course beckons. Apply your newly acquired knowledge, and let's play golf.

THE ANCIENT HOLES

No. 11 Saint Andrews, 172 Yards, Par 3

The Old Course, plain to the eye, vulnerable to the elements, intriguing to the shot maker, mystical to the pilgrim and initiate alike, Royal and Ancient to all. These traits converge at the par-3 eleventh hole. An elevated, shallow green is guarded by the deep and dreadful Strath bunker in front and the greedy Hill bunker to the left. After you've assessed the variable winds blowing off the

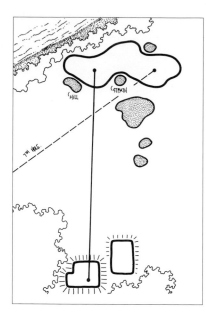

The Strath and Hill bunkers make this seemingly harmless hole, which crosses the seventh fairway, a challenge for any golfer.

Eden Estuary, hit and hope that your ball finds the putting surface. If it doesn't, now your real strategy begins on this penal hole.

The cup is usually cut close behind the Strath bunker, which swallows any mishit shot like a dragon. Only Saint George can enter and expect to escape safely from this sod-revetted hell. Guarding the green to the left is the less devilish yet troublesome Hill bunker. During the third round of the 1921 British Open, after a 46 on the first nine, the great Bobby Jones found himself in the Hill bunker. Facing a short putt for a "horrid 6," he said to himself, "What's the use?," picked up his ball, and walked off the course.

The only comfort found here is that the glassy green slopes upward at the back. This solace soon proves illusory to anyone who, blasting too far, must execute a downhill chip, which rapidly causes a sense of desperation as the golfer watches it accelerate past the cup to reenter the dreaded bunker. Back on the green, three-putts are the norm, especially for the already unnerved player. The rule of life was hard, and golf reflects that in Scotland. Here is found the true Gospel of Golf, where fate and luck are your constant playing companions. Despite its age, the Old Course continues to withstand the test of time, technology, and the world's greatest players.

No. 15 North Berwick, 192 Yards, Par 3

The Redan hole has had an important impact because many architects have copied or used the principle of a diagonal green throughout the twentieth century. The original Redan was a fortification fronted by long, deep trenches that defended Sebastopol during the Crimean War. The hole that bears its name at North Berwick, Scotland, requires a different strategy each day because of its configuration; deep, unforeseen sand bunkers; and variable wind. The green slopes downward from front to back and is angled diagonally from front right to back left, offering a limited view of the flag. A deep bunker guards the left side, while several smaller bunkers protect the right side.

Club selection must be accurate (usually an extra club from front to back), but bold shots may not hold the putting surface. Many players try a billiard-type shot aimed at the strong mound on the safer right side of the green, relying upon it to bank the ball toward the center of the putting surface. But beware if the pin is positioned on the left. Safe plays will result in difficult putts, or worse, the ball may end up in the grassy hollows beyond, which requires a delicate chip, to be executed with finesse, to the sloping green.

The fourth hole at the National Golf Links in Southampton, New York, by Charles Blair Macdonald is a fine rendition of this hole, as are the second at Somerset Hills in New Jersey by A. W. Tillinghast, the fourth at High Pointe Golf Club in Michigan by Tom Doak, and the fifteenth at Poppy Hills on the Monterey Peninsula. A modern use of the Redan principle with water replacing the left bunker is the downhill twelfth at Spyglass Hill.

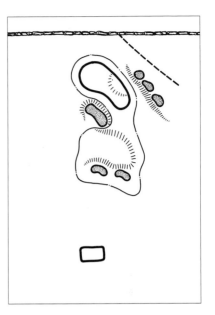

The original Redan hole, the par-3 fifteenth at North Berwick in Scotland, features a diagonal green that falls away in the rear with a large, deep hazard fronting it.

EARLY TWENTIETH CENTURY

No. 5 Royal Portrush, 389 Yards, Par 4

This Northern Ireland course was laid out in 1888 and extensively remodeled by H. S. Colt many years later. Harry Colt was an educated man, a lawyer by training and practice. He was the first Club Secretary at Sunningdale outside London, and an excellent amateur player who applied his golfing knowledge to the landscape's potential. Colt liked to play low clipped shots for his approaches. Thus, the new greens he designed rewarded shots punched under the wind along the ground, skirting the bunkers, mounds, and hollows flanking green entrances. Airy pitches would sail in the gusty ocean winds, and untrue run-up shots would climb up and then fall off into one of these guardian bunkers or hollows.

The fifth hole, while invitingly beautiful, is without the visual terror of even one of the deep pot bunkers found elsewhere on the course. But beware, this tiger, seemingly toothless, yields par only

grudgingly. Two comfortable shots should find the green set high on a seaside dune. But after a downhill tee shot to an ample fairway, it is very difficult to judge the correct distance and the appropriate club required on the second shot. The ball frequently pitches back from the green or overflies it, leaving the overconfident golfer bewildered. Now deft chipping and putting on this beautifully subtle green is the only hope or the golfer will leave the hole with a bogey or worse and overwhelming regret.

This wonderful hole, superbly crafted by Colt, illustrates that while the absence of water and bunkers may cause little tension on the approach, the shot cannot be taken for granted. In fact, the illusory effect and lack of definition around the green, with its glistening ocean background distracting the eye, make it imperative to put forth extra effort to determine the actual yardage.

No. 13 Pine Valley, 446 Yards, Par 4

Pine Valley was conceived by the generous sportsman George Crump, who largely carried out the work in the rolling New Jersey

Pine Barrens near Clementon. He was assisted by H. S. Colt, who drew the routing of the course and collaborated on the design of the detailed features.

It's a place of dark sparkling ponds and fresh springs once used by Native Americans. The character of the land, formed when the sea receded aeons ago, is now covered by fast-growing pines and colorful deciduous trees. The course evokes a sandy remembrance of an ancient time and is now a special haven reserved for golfers only. Its layout features island fairways and calls for aerial golf shots played over sandy wasteland to lush fairways and greens.

The thirteenth, a long par-4, requires an uphill tee shot across a deep swale to a crowned fairway, where hooked shots carom into natural sandy hollows and pot bunkers, and slices end up in the piney woods.

Standing over your second shot, notice the offset fairway to the right, bracketed on left and far right for 100 yards by a series of artful grass and sand bunkers, flowing to a huge, almost square green. Often, it is best to play safe to the ample lower level fairway and then chip to the open fall-away green from that angle to gain a better chance at a par or sure bogey. A good strategy for the average golfer is not to be seduced into going for the green when the odds are against success. Weigh the alternatives and play the percentages.

The direct approach to the green requires a heroic downhill shot. This hole is also penal: a mishit may never be recovered, and a cautious player may take several chips and putts and conclude with a double-bogey without missing a shot. The brave player will feel the exhilaration of success if the ball lands safely after carrying a series of penal bunkers. In my opinion, it is the best heroic hole in the eastern United States.

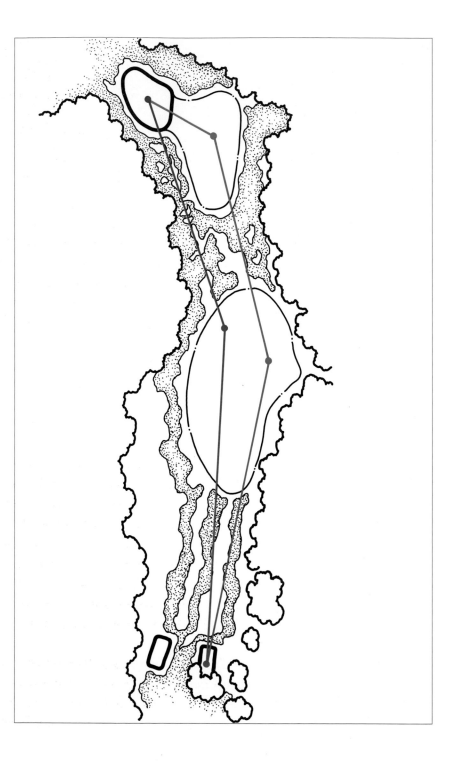

Long considered symbolic of the penal design school, Pine Valley's par-4 thirteenth hole requires precise shot making, or doom awaits.

No. 5 Mid Ocean, 433 Yards, Par 4

Bermuda's Mid Ocean fifth hole, known as the Cape Hole, presents golfers with one of the game's great risk-reward challenges. When you approach the tee, you get a first glimpse of one of the most truly heroic tee shots ever conceived. A jagged inlet known as Mangrove Lake has been incorporated at a diagonal angle to the line of the tee shot on this lengthy, gentle dogleg to the left. The golfers' real difficulty lies in the need for (I) a correct determination of the carry they can handle in order to select a proper line for that day's wind and (2) an objective assessment of their own abilities regarding execution of the stroke they have chosen to attempt.

The large, wide fairway that slopes from right to left toward the water's edge affords golfers a safety or bail-out area to the right. The penal finality associated with the large water hazard will surely cause many to choose this alternative, but at a great loss in both angle and distance to complete the remainder of the hole. Standing on this tee will prompt a faster pulse rate.

Assuming the drive has been successfully negotiated, you are left with a fairly long approach along a fairway that gradually slopes toward the lake on the left. If you decide to lay up, play to the right, as the ball will roll toward the water hazard. Bunkers bracket the green on both sides, leaving you the option to bounce your shot into the green. As with most C. B. Macdonald putting surfaces, the green features pronounced continuous slope, and the angle of attack becomes vital in order to place the ball near the pin. Therefore, the left edge of the fairway is ideal for any approach, but the risk remains ever present because the water hazard tightly guards this side.

This exceptional design was conceived late in his career by the patriarch of American golf course architecture, C. B. Macdonald, who was assisted on many projects by Seth Raynor and Charles Banks. Macdonald's courses were generous in all their elements. They featured wide fairways, multitudes of bunkers, and oversized greens with radical contours. His other prominent work includes the Chicago Golf Club, the National Golf Links, and the Yale University Golf Course.

THE CLASSICAL ERA

No. 6 Seminole, 390 Yards, Par 4

Florida golf is manicured green grass etched by wind, sun, sand, and salt water. Seminole, hard by the dunes margin of the Atlantic, attracts sun worshipers and golfers alike.

The par-4 sixth was one of Ben Hogan's favorite holes. In the days before aerodynamically dimpled balls and high-tech clubs, only the most skilled players like Hogan could work and place the

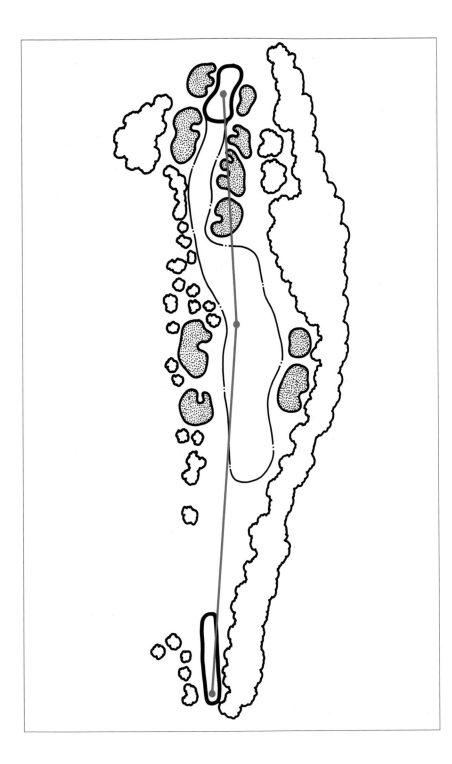

*Proper positioning off the tee is
imperative to tame the par-4 sixth
hole at Seminole Golf Club in
Palm Beach, Florida.*

ball into position for their next shot. The sixth demanded the best of even the expert players to reach the green in two.

The hole doglegs slightly to the left, and careful placement of bunkers throughout makes thoughtful shot making a must. The optimum angle of approach to the putting surface is from the left side of the fairway; but the player who chooses this line can be penalized by the extensive and formidable bunkering just to the left of the landing area. It is vintage Donald Ross. The narrow green has a receptive feeling but in reality demands an accurate and well-conceived approach to reach the putting surface, bunkered heavily in an indented diagonal fashion on the front right. Recovery from a poor approach will be difficult, another Ross trait. He was well known for greens that fell away at the edges of the putting surface, the ball spilling into a bunker or grassy hollow and presenting a difficult chip to recover.

Ross was a dour soul but polite and pleasant to the public. He was head professional at Pinehurst and was an accomplished player, often shooting his age in his seventies. Frequently, his work reflected his frugal nature: a minimal amount of design and field work to complete a new course. On request, Ross often designed simple courses on farms, but his masterpiece was Pinehurst No. 2 in North Carolina.

No. 13 Baltusrol, 383 Yards, Par 4

A. W. Tillinghast is one of my favorite architects. His conceptions were site specific. That is, he adapted the golf features, such as the depth of the bunkers, to the soil and terrain conditions of the property.

At Winged Foot in Mamaroneck, New York, he had a rocky site, so the greens were elevated and the bunkers steep-faced into them. You know right away you must fly the ball over the bunkers; don't even think of hitting a run-up shot at Winged Foot. At San

THE PAR-4 THIRTEENTH AT BALTUSROL GOLF CLUB IN SPRINGFIELD, NEW JERSEY, IS A FINE EXAMPLE OF A DOGLEG HOLE WITH A DIAGONAL WATER HAZARD THAT TEMPTS PLAYERS TO CHALLENGE IT.

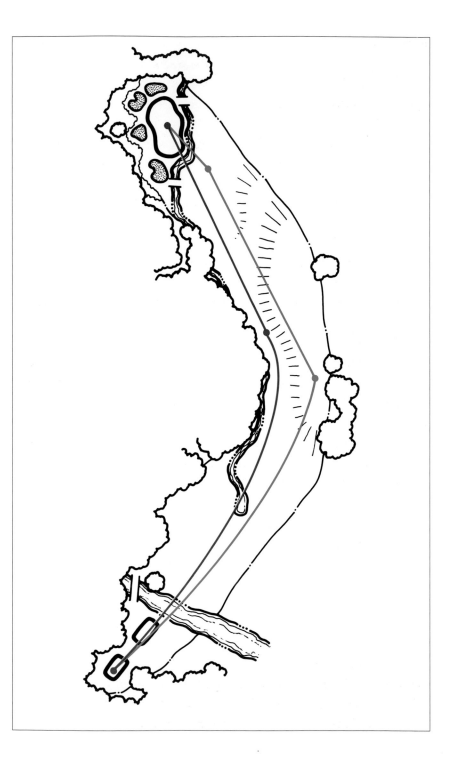

To get the best of No. 13 at Augusta, golfers must play close to Rae's Creek off the tee, and again near the green.

Francisco Golf Club, he had a sandy site that drained naturally, so he depressed many of his large, sweeping fairway and greenside bunkers below the original ground level and used them to create illusions.

His fairways arced rather than doglegged, and the bunkers usually lured the risk taker because they rarely bracketed the target area. Rather, they indented into the fairway, tempting a carry shot. He was an artful architect with a keen strategic sense and a wonderful golfing soul.

The thirteenth at Baltusrol in Springfield, New Jersey, is a dogleg par-4 requiring a carry over a brook, which crosses on a diagonal from short left to far right. Play left and a longer and more difficult second shot ensues. A hooked shot will find a fairway bunker or rough. It is best to aim at the target bunker and hit a power fade. Play down the creek line and the ball hangs ominously over the water hazard close to the trees, although a shorter second shot will result. This is an equitable hole, rewarding risk taking while testing courage and confidence off the tee. The remaining approach is straightforward with bracketing greenside bunkers snaring any misdirected shots. The green is ample and bell-shaped with fast-paced but subtle crowned contours.

Baltusrol is well suited to the USGA philosophy of corridor fairways with tough rough to test the accuracy and length of the game's best players. That is why it continues to attract many important championships.

No. 13 Augusta National, 485 Yards, Par 5

Augusta National — the very name evokes images of azaleas, dogwoods, glasslike greens, and great championships. Home of the Masters, the tournament celebrates the first rite of spring and is beloved by fans around the world for its dramatic finishes.

This Georgia course was coauthored by Robert Tyre Jones, Jr., and Dr. Alister Mackenzie, who attempted to replicate certain links-style features of the Old Course at St. Andrews on the rolling Georgia pine land. What first evolved was a sprawling, parkland layout that dwarfed the Old Course in size, but which retained the charm and playing character of its Scottish inspiration.

The heart and soul of the course are the par-5s, especially the thirteenth, a classic heroic hole. Concluding a difficult stretch of holes, known as Amen Corner, this subtle dogleg left makes marvelous use of the sloping terrain, which banks gently from right to left. The hole requires a slightly uphill tee shot and provides a textbook example of how to use water on the inside of a dogleg to tempt golfers to choose a line that will shorten distance. Greedy players who cut off too much yardage are likely to find Rae's Creek, which flanks the entire left side of the hole and meanders in front of the large, flowing green to gobble up misplayed second shots or sloppy approaches.

The thirteenth is a classic example of integrating topographical features into a natural setting. It is easy to become lulled into a false sense of security by the florid beauty and graceful bunkering, but the hole is no pushover. Mackenzie was a master of camouflage, and these distractions are a good example. The green looks inviting and tempts you to attack it. Even if you succeed, the contoured putting surface will test your touch and nerves.

HARD TIMES AND POSTWAR RENAISSANCE

No. 14 Banff Springs, 210 Yards, Par 3

Stanley Thompson was a charming, persuasive nonconformist and artist, who could steal your heart as well as your par. He came from a distinguished family of golfers — four brothers were amateur or professional champions. Stanley was the golf architect. His brothers attacked the game, and he provided the elusive targets. Thompson, an outstanding Canadian designer, was my father's mentor during the depression.

Stanley Thompson's courses throughout Canada and the northern United States are works of golf art. He loved natural landscapes, and his large, sweeping bunkers emulated the seaside dunes even in the high Canadian Rockies at Banff and Jasper. He was known for his strong par-4s and charming par-3s, but his three-shot par-5s have given way to the technical advances of today's equipment.

The 210-yard fourteenth hole at Banff Springs, nicknamed Little Bow, is a long, narrow par-3 played along the wide and rushing Bow River to a large green. What makes it a difficult shot is the wind, which reverberates off the mountains and is ever swirling. Drop a handkerchief at the tee and a gentle zephyr might carry it slightly to the right, but look at the flag and it is blowing stiff to the left. Here the invisible hazard is a wicked wind, requiring cunning and a sixth sense to fathom its effect on club selection and the type of shot required: sometimes a high, long, floating shot; at other times, a low knockdown shot that bores through the wind.

In the east, trees are the third dimension. In the wide, open west, the towering mountain settings add scale, and the courses are grand with oversized features. Large greens need massive bunkers in a wilderness setting. Banff Springs has it all.

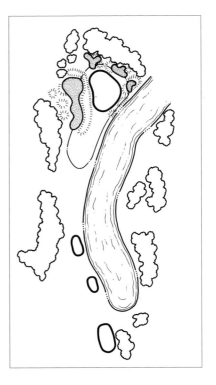

Selecting the correct club is vital to staying dry on the par-3 fourteenth hole at Banff Springs in Alberta, Canada.

No. 4 Spyglass Hill, 376 Yards, Par 4

My father's work is known for long "runway" tees, fairways that extend from tee to green framed with large bunkers, and expansive, contoured, elevated greens. He intentionally made his courses difficult, and every par is well earned. A stimulating mix of these features awaits the golfer at Spyglass Hill's inland forest holes (Nos. 6 through 18), which are solid and formidable golfing challenges.

However, the measure of a truly fine architect rests with his ability to sometimes go against his own tendencies in favor of creating a special hole. In my father's case, the fourth is the antithesis of his basic design principles. It sits like a crown jewel in the midst of brilliant white sand dunes next to the glittering cobalt sea. The tee shot from any of the small individual tees on this short par-4 offers numerous options. As with the other dunescape holes in this golfing country, No. 4 is treeless and thereby vulnerable to the sometimes fierce sea winds. The driver is often replaced by a 3-wood or long iron because proper placement of the ball on the correct side of the fairway (usually the right) is rewarded with a preferred angle to this well-guarded punch-bowl green nestled deeply among the forbidding sand dunes.

From tee to green, the hole is surrounded by magnificent natural dunes. A mishit shot may as often as not fall victim to a tiny but lethal plant crowning these dunes: the dreaded ice plant. This nemesis is a great deal stronger than the fittest golfer. Often, after mighty swings, the ball remains as it was, apparent yet unmoved amid this tiny succulent. This condition provides enormous frustration to the player and can be disastrous to the score.

This possible fate makes a driver out of the question on windy days. Yet the green has been driven on occasion. The risk of driving into the narrow entrance in front of the green is not worth the chance. On the other hand, an overly cautious tee shot to a wider landing area will present a surprisingly difficult middle iron to a narrow, two-tiered, fall-away green. Attempting to stop the ball on this green with a hot approach shot is like trying to hold water with your bare hands.

The green's slopes, contours, and troughs will make completing this seemingly innocent hole just as challenging as starting it. The fourth at Spyglass Hill demonstrates a great architect's ability to adapt his design to the natural setting.

THE DEVELOPMENT ERA

No. 16 Harbour Town, 378 Yards, Par 4

Harbour Town on Hilton Head Island, South Carolina, is typical of a period when the holes of courses were spread apart to afford the integration of houses into the course. Pete Dye, an excellent golfer, left his insurance profession in the 1960s to pursue golf architecture as his vocation. Some of Pete's contributions to golf architecture are the use of wooden planks and railroad ties as decorative features for bunkers and contrasting grasses to create visual excitement and intimidating hazards. He has built a number of captivating short par-4s during his career, and the sixteenth at Harbour Town is one of his finest.

The tee shot is played out of a chute of trees to a fairway that doglegs sharply from right to left. With the tees being positioned in the woods, the golfer is likely to be unaware of the wind

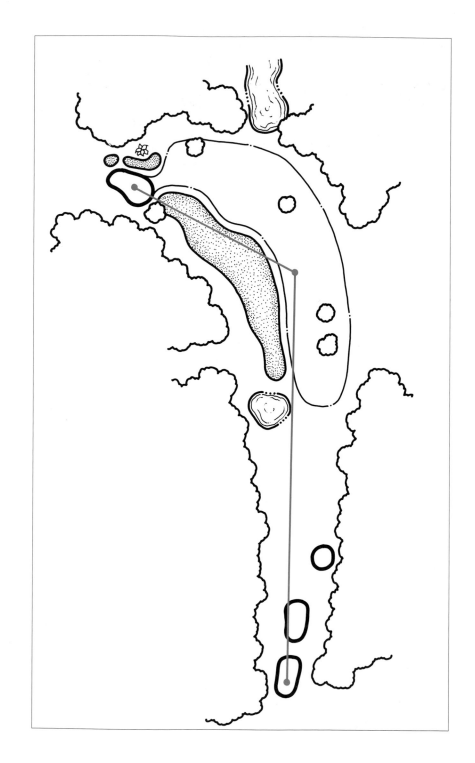

A massive sandy waste area guards the left side of the par-4 sixteenth at Harbour Town, which can play havoc with your score.

intensity beyond the trees. The breeze off Calibogue Sound, quartering from the left, can significantly affect the flight of the tee ball. The drive is further complicated by the large, unmaintained, sandy waste area that protects the hole's left side from the landing area all the way to the green. A large tree in the right center of the fairway functions as a target off the tee.

The ideal shot is to play close to the waste area and as far up the fairway as possible, leaving a short approach to the smallish green. However, golfers who choose to take this risk increase the chance that they may wind up in the waste area with a less than perfect lie and approach angle to the green. Many tour players use a 3-wood off the tee to ensure a good angle to the green. A safer drive to the right side will leave a longer and more difficult approach, while taking the waste area out of play. This waste-area hazard has the severe, hard edges for which Dye has become known.

The fairway is flat and lacks any tilt to help a shot turn with the angle of the dogleg. A shot lost to the right will leave you with a much longer approach to the green. The fairway wraps around the large banana-shaped waste area, leaving a small possibility for bouncing your approach shot into the green.

A single bunker protects the green on the right. A narrow neck of fairway tongue separates the entrance from the huge sandy waste defending the entire left side of the green. As with most smaller greens, recovery shots must be lobbed or lofted, and the surface is gentle, making putting a simpler task.

The sixteenth at Harbour Town is representative of Dye's early work. In my opinion, many of his courses after Harbour Town were exaggerated to be photogenic and newsworthy. The inspiration for his concepts came from a romantic attachment to ancient courses. However, his innovations and creativity have influenced many architects of our time, including Tom Fazio and Jack Nicklaus.

No. 13 Desert Highlands, 396 Yards, Par 4

Due to their consummate golfing skills, pros like to eliminate luck's impact on scoring. Courses designed by Jack Nicklaus often reflect this philosophy by providing extremely flat tees, preferred landing areas that are almost level, and pin positions with minimal contour. If you have the skill to reach these targets, you will enjoy level lies. The thirteenth hole at Desert Highlands in Scottsdale, Arizona, embodies all these features.

The course has many interesting holes, but this uphill par-4 is emblematic of Nicklaus, whose designs reflect a professional's deep understanding of shot values. The tee shot is played from one of five intimate, flat teeing areas. An arroyo splits the fairway into two separate landing areas, with the preferred, relatively level right side requiring a significant carry over the native desert floor. Players who desire a safer route can play up the wider left-side fairway but will face a longer and more difficult approach shot. The right side will afford a tremendous advantage on the ensuing stroke. There are options from the tee, and you must make an intelligent choice based on the conditions and your abilities.

Another trait you are likely to encounter when playing one of Jack's courses is that greens are set in a diagonal fashion. The thirteenth is situated diagonally from the front right to the back left and is defended with a large single bunker in front. This diagonal bunker is congruent with the green shape, thus requiring an approach shot from the left landing area to be an aerial one. A shot from the right-hand fairway provides a chance to bounce the ball onto the front of the green, which has been sloped to feed the ball from right to left. The approach also must factor in the gradual change in elevation, which is often misread on desert landscapes that contain few or no reference points.

The green is on the large side and slopes toward the rear perimeter, but the contour has been created more for the purpose of helping

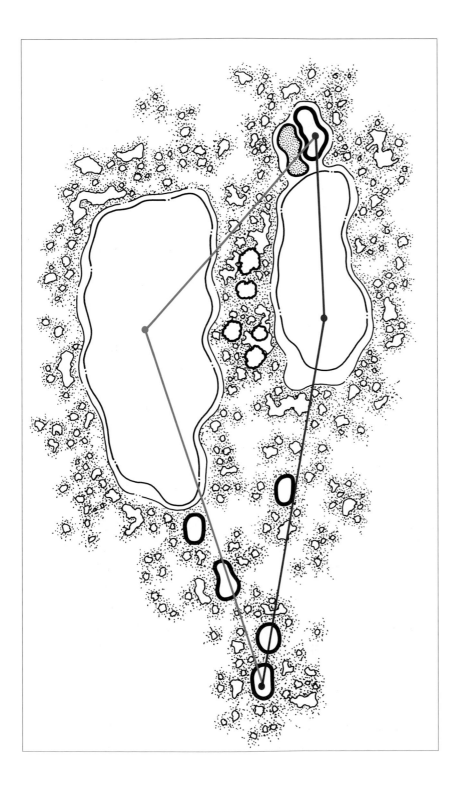

*The par-4 thirteenth hole at
Desert Highlands Golf Club in
Scottsdale, Arizona, gives players two
distinct options off the tee.*

a good approach shot than to affect putting. Nicklaus hits high approach shots, and his greens are well designed to receive them. The pinnable areas are relatively flat, especially considering that the natural movement of the surrounding terrain is somewhat sloping. The green area also contains some mounding, which is developed largely for backdrop. The thirteenth is a fine example of utilizing the native desert to its fullest.

The rough at Desert Highlands is a modern adaptation of Pine Valley's natural wasteland concept. You can recover from the sand transition areas, but beware of the dangerous cactus and wildlife of the open desert beyond. The wasteland rough approach conforms to the new water conservation laws for the parched Arizona desert.

The Environmental Era

No. 13 Black Diamond Ranch, 183 Yards, Par 3

Tom Fazio has produced a number of fine courses, and his work over the past decade reflects another trend in golf course architecture during the modern era — that of visual aesthetics. As many landscape architectural students have come into the profession of golf course architecture, they have influenced the look of golf courses. This is clearly evident in the work of Fazio and his talented staff.

I found the thirteenth hole at Black Diamond in Lecanto, Florida, to be fascinating. The 183-yard hole is played from elevated tees across a deep, abandoned limestone quarry. As with many forced carries, the shot-making requirement is less demanding than it appears. A tiny area of fairway and two bunkers guarding the left edge of the green provide a possible bail-out area, with the majority of trouble lurking short and right. When viewed from the tee, a large, deep, slightly cocked green sits on a plateau with four

bunkers surrounding it. The two left bunkers are large, sprawling hazards that allow an easier recovery to the putting surface. The front and right bunkers have much sharper edges, making escape more difficult.

The double-tiered putting surface is comprised of two distinct pinning areas. Golfers must factor the great depth of the green into their club selection. The pinnable areas are relatively flat, but the up-and-over transition can make for many interesting possibilities when chipping, pitching, or putting from one deck to another. This component type of green typifies Fazio's style of larger putting surfaces broken up by significant contour.

The hole is dramatic and fun, and it embodies the principles of an exciting setting with demanding golf shots. While neither long nor intimidating, it is a hole you look forward to playing.

SIMILAR TO JOONDALUP'S THIRD HOLE, A DEEP QUARRY SERVES AS A DRAMATIC HAZARD ON THE PAR-3 THIRTEENTH HOLE AT BLACK DIAMOND RANCH IN LECANTO, FLORIDA.

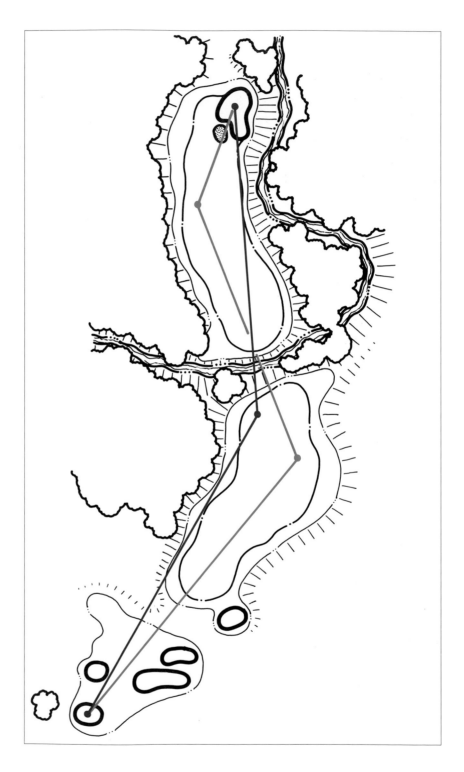

The presence of the twisting ravine makes the par-5 fifteenth on the Prince Course at Princeville a thrill from tee to green.

No. 15 The Prince Course, 576 Yards, Par 5

Occasionally, an architect is fortunate to be presented with a magnificent site that presents tremendous opportunities. When this happens, there is a tingle in the golfing nerves. I have been blessed to work on several great pieces of dramatic property, including the land now known as Highland Springs in Missouri; Keystone in Colorado; The National in Australia; Pine Lake in Japan; The Links at Spanish Bay in Pebble Beach; Sugarloaf in Maine; Chateau Whistler in British Columbia; and Golf Club de Grenoble in France.

Certainly the bluffs overlooking the Pacific Ocean and the huge ravine, with waterfalls and streams amid the mature tropical vegetation, place the Prince Course at Princeville, Hawaii, in that glorious assemblage. Due to local environmental regulations, the course had to be built in three- and four-hole increments, providing ample time to craft subtle details into each hole. The Prince Course contains a number of challenging and memorable holes, but the fifteenth captures both the shot-making strategies and the aesthetics of the property to the fullest.

The tees are situated on the crest of a hill far above the rolling landing area. This cascading descent is formidable and must be taken into account when choosing a club for the drive. Long hitters could reach the gorge that parallels the fairway on the left and then bisects the fairway to separate the first and second landing areas. The initial landing area is wide and friendly, although the hazard running down the left side will catch an unplanned hook. Mogul-like mounding is abundant in the fairway, which tilts downhill and from right to left. The ball will roll and slow through these mounds until it rests. Within the hole, I strive to craft features that flow and blend together.

When the first landing area is reached, the drama of the hole unfolds and comes into clear view. The remainder is dominated

FOLLOWING PAGE:
FROM THE ELEVATED TEE, THE
ROLLING, SWEEPING CHARACTER OF
THE PRINCE'S FIFTEENTH IS AN
EXHILARATING EXPERIENCE, ESPECIALLY
WHEN YOU FIND THE FAIRWAY.

by the large ravine that flanks the entire right side. It must be avoided at all costs on both the second and subsequent shots. The second landing area is amply wide but paralleled by tropical vegetation and a steep hill on the left. A single pot bunker, the only one on the hole, is perfectly positioned to protect the green — which itself abuts the deep chasm. Choosing the risky line can yield great reward. As with the entire course, clear edges allow golfers to choose precisely the degree of risk they are willing to take.

The green surface is small and requires accuracy. Because of its minimal size, the green contains only minor degrees of subtle slope. Golfers must be careful to factor in the grain associated with tropical bermudagrass putting surfaces. The fifteenth is a spectacular, heroic par-5 that can be reached with two perfect shots, yet it provides an abundance of shot-making decisions for a player of any skill.

Composing the Symphony

If we replicated the fourteen holes we have just looked at and added four more excellent holes at random, would we have one of golfdom's best courses? Almost certainly not. Most likely we would have a golf course with an unpleasing mood and pace, much like a symphony created by tacking together measures from famous pieces. All great courses do, however, possess an overall mood or rhythm that engenders feelings of anticipation mixed with nostalgia in most players when they reflect on the course.

The architect produces this effect in a fashion similar to the way in which a composer creates a great symphony. Each hole is deftly adapted to the site's natural attributes — a green configuration appropriate for a tropical forest probably would be a poor choice for a windy, open links site. A great course also has balance, which derives from the melding, in a pleasing order, of holes of varying degrees of difficulty. If every hole were extremely challenging, it would be like listening to a symphony where every note was played

at maximum volume and every measure was at breakneck speed. The constant intensity would soon overwhelm the sensitivities of listeners and golfers alike.

There are no absolute rules for sequencing pars or musical notes, and some great courses feature unusual combinations. Take, for instance, Cypress Point on the Monterey Peninsula, which has back-to-back par-3s and back-to-back par-5s, or nearby Poppy Hills, with five par-3s and five par-5s. A pleasing and often encountered structure starts with a less challenging getaway hole, and a par-3 usually doesn't appear until the third or fourth hole. The most intricate and challenging holes occur in the middle of the course, followed by a breather or two setting the stage for an intense, dramatic finale.

For me the hallmark of a great course resides in a golfer's ability to remember and visualize all the holes after playing the course once. This is possible only if the architect has harmoniously blended

CYPRESS POINT CLUB, RENOWNED AS ONE OF THE GREAT GOLF COURSES IN THE WORLD, FEATURES BACK-TO-BACK PAR-3S AT THE FIFTEENTH AND SIXTEENTH HOLES.

eighteen holes, each of which, regardless of its degree of difficulty, is memorable and stimulating.

What is it about certain golf courses that calls you back to play them time and again? Is it that they reward you with pleasure commensurate with your skills? Long ago Alister Mackenzie observed that the player derived much more pleasure by overcoming a difficult challenge with a great shot than playing a bland, uninteresting course and achieving a low score. There is nothing quite like the wonderful feeling of exhilaration that comes from hitting a full-blooded 4-wood over the inlet of Carmel Bay to the small green on the eighth hole of Pebble Beach.

There is a great sense of relief and more than a modicum of pleasure derived when, after your approach shot finds a greenside bunker, you successfully get it out near enough to the hole to make a good putt to save a par. However, this pleasure is a far cry from the euphoria resulting from a perfectly executed heroic shot. Making a good medal score for a round close to your handicap is pleasurable, but even more so on a course tougher than your home club.

Many players think these positive vibrations derive from a mastery of swing mechanics. However, as soon as you advance beyond the restless quest for the elusive perfect swing, you begin to think about the golf course itself.

Sometimes the course yields, and at other times it has you in one of its hazards. But does it? It is great fun to escape from difficulty and play on. When you begin to ask why a particular bunker is small or a shallow bunker is not deeper, you are beginning to think about strategy.

Did the designer consider the prevailing wind and the flow of the holes? Did he pick the best green sites and design the hole backward to the tee area? Did the architect fit the course to the land given to him or did he ignore it and impose a preconceived concept on the blank canvas he was offered?

When you raise these questions, you are getting inside the golf architect's mind, and it can be endlessly fascinating. Most of all, you are learning to create an attack for his defenses and you are becoming a true shot maker. This is what the game of golf is all about.

I believe that a golf course is a great urban park — it's the lungs of a city. When you fly into Chicago, Miami, or Los Angeles, you'll see green spaces and suburbs that have grown up around them. More often than not, these pockets are golf courses. Not only do they provide oxygenation, but they also serve as wildlife habitats and bird sanctuaries.

In recent years there has been increasing concern about the effect of golf courses on the environment. Issues involving endangered species, wetlands, pesticides, and other related topics are hotly debated.

Virtually every scientific concern raised can be overcome by a competent architect if the owner provides enough usable land. For example, at the Windsor Club in Vero Beach, Florida, we incorporated local native grasses, which provided herons and other birds a sanctuary not previously available. The Audubon Society of New York now assists courses that have adopted this attitude. At the Squaw Creek Golf Course in Olympic Valley, California, we restored an abused and forsaken meadow while carefully integrating holes among the mountain wetlands. At The Orchards, a public golf course north of Detroit, Michigan, a natural-gas storage field has been utilized for golf. For those who don't want to walk the course, the owners are now building natural-gas golf carts, which emit far fewer pollutants into the air.

THE RESORT AT SQUAW
CREEK HARMONIZES WITH ITS
SURROUNDING ENVIRONMENT.

In addition, the turf grass associated with a golf course provides numerous benefits beyond oxygenation, including noise abatement, pollutant absorption, temperature modification, and a buffer zone against wildfires, to name only a few.

What does this mean to the ordinary golfer? Natural golfscapes have returned. Where you once paid for an errant shot with a bogey, you'll now pay an environmental "green fee" with cash — should you decide to search for the ball. At Spanish Bay, it's a misdemeanor to walk in sensitive areas.

When I first learned the fundamentals of golf course architecture during my early years in the profession, spacious property was more available. In the early 1970s, when Hawaiian golf course development was still in its early stages, I was fortunate to work with spectacular land on the northern side of Kauai, now known as Princeville Resort. It consisted of a series of magnificent bluffs overlooking the Pacific Ocean. Land like that is scarce, especially today. On the rare occasion you find a great piece of property, obtaining the necessary permits can be more difficult than playing from the championship tees. But as we have learned, patience and virtue are rewarded in the end.

Advancements in equipment have had a major impact on how architects think about the game. High-tech shafts, perimeter-weighted clubheads, and livelier balls have led to increases in distance, which has rendered some classical courses obsolete for major tournament play. This has primarily occurred off the tee, where fairway bunkers no longer pose the same challenge as in their original design because most players can carry them easily. We architects will build new championship tees and sometimes put a little governor on the engines of long hitters by integrating crossbunkering or tightening landing areas.

Golf is headed in many directions, and the more the merrier. I've built courses around the world, in newly developed countries from Indonesia and mainland China at Shanghai, to the Transkei in Southern Africa. I've worked in the Pacific Rim from Mexico to Japan and Australia to Thailand, and from England, France, Portugal and Finland to Russia.

Building Moscow Country Club has been a once-in-a-lifetime experience, difficult to accomplish but immensely satisfying. The golf course is situated at Nahabino, northwest of Moscow in a beautiful, mature forest studded with tall evergreens and birch trees on a gently rolling site. Nine holes were planted in the fall of 1992 and, when completed, it will be the first 18-hole championship golf course in Russia.

While the game's popularity continues to climb, countries like England, Japan, Canada, and even the United States simply don't have enough courses to support its growth. Municipalities, counties, states, and private entrepreneurs must collaborate in a cohesive manner to produce more public facilities, or potential golfers will either lose interest or be left out in the cold.

One trend that disturbs me is the penchant for remodeling, especially traditional courses. Closely examined, this usually results in taking what were classical greens and destroying them, mainly from misunderstanding. You wouldn't remodel a Frank Lloyd Wright house. While it is true that a golf course is a work in progress — trees grow and the like — the essence and intent of a classic layout ought to be preserved.

In reading this book, you have, I hope, gained a better appreciation for the mental side of the game. An architect has a specific intention when creating a golf course, and your challenge is to decipher it and then proceed accordingly. Further, I hope that now, instead of hurrying to the first tee and swinging away, you will formulate a specific game plan for each course and stick to it. Not only will you lower your score, but you'll have more fun.

My purpose in writing this book has been to help you get the most out of the course by knowing how to attack it. But remember, no golfer is completely satisfied, not even the professionals. Each round is different, and smart players learn from their mistakes.

I marvel at the old Scots who can make pars without getting the ball airborne. For more than five hundred years, they have negotiated sprawling links, sand dunes, and bunkers without yardage markers or fancy scorecards. Their only allies have been their eyes and experience.

When you think about it, golf is really a simple game. It hasn't changed much from the early days when sheep roamed the course. The object is still to get a tiny ball into a small hole in as few strokes as possible. It's just that the obstacles have become more complex, making the game a greater challenge than ever before. However, if you utilize the principles I have set forth in this book, your chances for scoring success should increase dramatically. Play away!

DOMESTIC

ALASKA

Eagleglen Golf Course, Anchorage **(C)**

ARIZONA

The Oakcreek Country Club of Sedona, Sedona **(C)**

Rio Rico Resort & Country Club, Rio Rico

ARKANSAS

Chenal Country Club, Little Rock

CALIFORNIA

Adobe Creek Golf & Country Club, Petaluma

Birnam Wood Golf Club, Montecito **(C)**

Bodega Harbour Golf Links, Bodega Bay

Brookside Country Club, Stockton

Calabasas Park Golf & Country Club, Calabasas **(C)**

Coto de Caza Golf Club, Coto de Caza

Desert Dunes Golf Club, Desert Hot Springs

Forest Meadows Golf Course, Calaveras County

Laguna Seca Golf Club, Monterey **(C)**

Lake Shastina Resort (36 holes), Weed

Menlo Country Club, Woodside **(RC)**

Monarch Beach Golf Links, Monarch Beach

Poppy Hills (N.C.G.A.), Pebble Beach

Rancho California Golf Club, Murietta **(C)**

Rancho La Quinta Golf Club, La Quinta

Shoreline Golf Links, Mountain View

Silverado Country Club (North Course), Napa **(RC, C)**

Silverado Country Club (South Course), Napa

The Links at Spanish Bay, Pebble Beach **(CL)**

Spring Valley Lake Country Club, Victorville **(C)**

The Resort at Squaw Creek, Olympic Valley

COLORADO

Arrowhead Golf Club, Roxborough Park

Beaver Creek Golf Course, Avon

Keystone Ranch Golf Course, Keystone

Skyland Country Club, Crested Butte

Steamboat Golf Club & Resort, Steamboat Springs

FLORIDA

Kensington Golf Club, Naples

Weston Hills Country Club, Ft. Lauderdale

The Windsor Club, Vero Beach

HAWAII

Kiahuna Golf Village, Poipu Beach, Kauai

Makena Golf Resort (36 holes), Maui

Poipu Bay Resort Golf Course, Poipu Beach, Kauai

Princeville Prince Course, Princeville, Kauai

Princeville Makai Course (27 holes), Princeville, Kauai

Waikoloa Beach Golf Club, Waikoloa Village, Hawaii

Waikoloa Village Golf Course, Waikoloa Village, Hawaii

Wailea Golf Resort (Gold Course), Wailea, Maui

Wailea Golf Resort (Orange Course), Wailea, Maui

IDAHO

Elkhorn at Sun Valley, Sun Valley **(C)**

Sun Valley Resort, Sun Valley **(RC)**

ILLINOIS

Crystal Tree Golf Club, Orland Park

Prairie Landing Golf Club, West Chicago

KANSAS

Crestview Country Club (South Course 9-hole add.), Wichita

Deer Creek Golf Course, Overland Park

LOUISIANA

Le Triomphe Golf & Country Club, Lafayette

MAINE

Sugarloaf Golf Club, Carrabassett Valley

MICHIGAN

The Orchards Golf Club, Detroit

MINNESOTA

Edinburgh USA, Brooklyn Park

MISSOURI

Highland Springs Country Club, Springfield

NEVADA

Incline Village Golf Resort (Executive Course), Lake Tahoe

Lakeridge Golf Course, Reno **(C)**

Spanish Trail Golf & Country Club (27 holes), Las Vegas

NEW MEXICO

Cochiti Lake Golf Course, Cochiti Lake

NORTH DAKOTA

Oxbow Country Club, Oxbow

OHIO

Jefferson Golf & Country Club, Columbus

Wedgewood Golf & Country Club, Columbus

OREGON

Eugene Country Club, Eugene **(C)**

Heron Lakes Golf Course (Green-back Course), Portland

Heron Lakes Golf Course (Great Blue Course), Portland

Sunriver Resort (North Course), Sunriver

TEXAS

Horseshoe Bay Resort (Slickrock Course), Horseshoe Bay

Las Colinas Sports Club (original 18 holes), Irving

Mill Creek Golf & Country Club, Salado

VIRGINIA

Lansdowne Golf Resort, Leesburg

WISCONSIN

SentryWorld Golf, Stevens Point

University Ridge Golf Course, Madison

WYOMING

Jackson Hole Golf & Tennis Club, Jackson Hole **(C)**

INTERNATIONAL

ARUBA

Tierra del Sol Golf Club

AUSTRALIA

The Cape Golf Club, Cape Schanck, Melbourne

Hyatt Regency Coolum Golf Course, Sunshine Coast

Joondalup Country Club (27 holes), Perth

Meadow Springs, Mandurah, Western Australia

The National, Cape Schanck, Melbourne area

CANADA

Chateau Whistler Golf Course, Whistler, British Columbia

Glencoe Golf & Country Club (36 holes), Calgary, Alberta

CHINA

Shanghai Country Club, Shanghai

ENGLAND

The Wisley Golf Club (27 holes), Surrey

FIJI

Pacific Harbour Golf Course, Deuba

FINLAND

Ruuhikoski Golf Course, Nurmo

FRANCE

Club de Bondues (10 new holes), Lille

Golf & Country Club de Bossey, Haute Savoie

Golf Club de Grenoble, Grenoble

Saint Donat Golf Country Club, Cannes-Grasse

Vidauban Golf Course, Var **(C)**

HONG KONG

Discovery Bay Golf Club (original 18 holes), Lantau Island

INDONESIA

Pantai Indah Kapuk Golf Course, Jakarta

Pondok Indah Country Club, Jakarta Selatan

JAPAN

Cherry Hills Golf Club (27 holes), Miki, Hyōgo

The Country Club, Shigaraki, Shiga

Eastwood Golf Club, Tochigi

Golden Valley Golf Club, Nishiwaki, Hyōgo

Karuizawa Golf 72 (four 18-hole courses), Karuizawa, Gumma

Katsura Golf Course, Hokkaidō

King Hills Country Club, Kumamoto

Kinojo Golf Club, Okayama

Miho Country Club, Ibaraki

Nasu Highland Golf & Country Club, Tochigi

Oak Hills Country Club, Chiba

Onuma Prince Country Club, Hokkaidō

Pine Lake Golf Club, Nishiwaki, Hyōgo

Regus Crest Golf Club (Royal Course), Hiroshima

Regus Crest Golf Club (Grand Course), Hiroshima

Sapporo Prince Golf Club (36 holes), Hokkaidō

Shizukuishi Golf Course (original 18 holes), Mt. Takakura

Springfield Golf Club, Tajimi, Gifu

Sun Hills Country Club (36 holes), Tochigi

Zuiryo Golf Club, Gifu

KOREA

Yong Pyeong Golf Club, Yong Pyeong Resort

MALAYSIA

Bukit Jambul Country Club, Penang

Desaru Resort, Johor

The Mines Golf & Country Club, Kuala Lumpur

MEXICO

Cabo Real Golf Club, Cabo San Lucas, Baja California

Club de Golf Palma Real, Ixtapa-Zihuatanejo, Guerrero

Cancun Pok-Ta-Pok Resort Course, Quintana Roo

PHILIPPINES

Alabang Golf & Country Club, Rizal

Calatagan Golf Course, Batangas

Canlubang Golf Course (36 holes), Laguna

Sta. Elena Golf & Country Club, Laguna

PORTUGAL

Penha Longa Golf Club, Sintra

RUSSIA

Moscow Country Club, Nahabino, Moscow

SINGAPORE

Raffles Country Club (36 holes)

SOUTH AFRICA

Wild Coast Country Club, Transkei

SPAIN

Club de Bonmont Terres Noves, Tarragona

TAIWAN

The Royal Country Club, Miaoli

Sun Rise Country Club, Yang Mei

THAILAND

Eastern Star Country Club, Ban Chang

Green Valley Country Club, Bangkok

Navatanee Golf Course, Bangkok

President Country Club (36 holes), Bangkok

Santiburi Golf Club, Chiang Rai

WEST INDIES

Four Seasons Resort, Nevis

RC: reconstructed

C: with Robert Trent Jones Sr. collaborating

CL: with Tom Watson and Frank "Sandy" Tatum

During my teenage years, the legendary Tommy Armour taught me sophisticated playing techniques at the Winged Foot Golf Club. He also recounted golf stories and the lore of Scotland. It was he who told me that individual features of golf courses were given names in Scotland because of their special character. For the first time I began to think of a golf course as having a personality. Thus, he planted the seed for this book in my golfing soul thirty-five years ago.

This book is a product of a cohesive effort by a number of exceptional people. I name only a few, but wish to thank all the others who have been so generous with their time and assistance.

First and foremost, I am indebted to my creative father and wise mother. They brought me into this world and then introduced me to the wonderful game of golf. I consider myself to be one of the luckiest people on earth because I enjoy designing and building golf courses, an endeavor which provides me greater satisfaction with each ensuing year. My wife, Claiborne, supplied constant encouragement and, moreover, served as an unofficial editor helping to smooth out the text.

One of the aspects I love most about the golf world is the people involved in it. Don Knott, Gary Linn, Bruce Charlton, and Kyle Phillips are not only four of the game's most talented architects but also stellar human beings. It has been a deep pleasure for me to work with them as individuals and as a team on our projects around the world. The book benefits greatly from their painstaking research and contributions. I also add my thanks to my assistant, Gudren Noonan, for her tireless efforts.

I also want to thank professional writer Bill Bruns, who helped me start defining the scope of the book. Of equal importance, Bill also introduced the concept of the book to Little, Brown and Company, whose editors, Jordan Pavlin and Karen Dane, provided critical insights that I sincerely appreciate. I also wish to thank Editor-in-Chief Bill Phillips for his faith and guidance throughout the creation of this book.

My good friend Mike Bartlett, a writer and critic, provided valuable assistance in the continuing process of fleshing out the early part of the book's profile.

The book benefited immensely from the comments of Brad Klein and Lorne Rubenstein. These first-rate golf writers gave me detailed and penetrating comments that resulted in clearer descriptions. They also helped immeasurably in checking the accuracy of facts. Many friends read the early drafts and provided excellent contributions. Bill Pollak, Ron Dalby, Paul Fullmer, and Al Furber were of particular help. Englishman Richard Wax's extensive knowledge regarding European courses and golf lore, coupled with his deft language skills, served to add a luster and a sense of tradition to the book.

In addition to the photos from our own library, the photographic work of renowned golf photographers John and Jeannine Henebry, Brian Morgan, and Tony Roberts has given the book a wonderful visual quality. Ty Butler, a member of my firm, produced most of the book's excellent drawings which serve to bring alive the principles and concepts described in the text. Graphic designers Mauricio Arias and Catherine Richards did a masterful job with the layout of this book.

Lastly, I wish to express my special thanks to three close friends. First, Steve Schroeder contributed enormously throughout, developing and organizing the information. Second, Mark Soltau, noted golf columnist, aided greatly in shaping the book into final form. Finally, I want to express sincere gratitude to my closest friend and advisor, Blake Stafford, who worked tirelessly toward the book's completion. I cannot thank him enough for all of his wisdom and dedication to this project.